Disciplining the Soul

Ibn Al-Jawzi (d. 597 AH)

Every breath we take is taking us closer to death. The time we spend in this world is short, the time we are held in our graves is long, and the punishment for following our lowly desires is calamitous.

Good Books

Search by ISBN to buy the correct book

Stories of the Prophets	ISBN: 9781643543888
Timeless Seeds of Advice	ISBN: 9781643544069
Diseases of the Hearts & Cures	ISBN 9781643544106
The Noble Quran (Arabic)	ISBN: 9781643543994
Koran (English: Easy to Read)	ISBN: 9781643540924
The Path to Guidance	ISBN: 9781643544052
Miracles of the Prophet	ISBN: 9781643544038
Seerah of Prophet Muhammad	ISBN: 9781643543222
Book on Islam and Marriage	ISBN: 9781073877140
Great Women of Islam	ISBN: 9781643543758
Stories of the Koran	ISBN: 9781095900796
The Purification of the Soul	ISBN: 9781643541389
Al-Fawaid: Wise Sayings	ISBN: 9781727812718
The Book of Hajj	ISBN: 9781072243335
40 Hadith Qudsi	ISBN: 9781070655949
40 Hadith Nawawi	ISBN: 9781070547428
The Legacy of the Prophet	ISBN: 9781080249343
The Ideal Muslim Woman	ISBN: 9781643543192
The Soul's Journey after Death	ISBN: 9781643541365
Ota Benga	ISBN: 9781643543802
Don't Be Sad	ISBN: 9781643543451
Khalid Bin Al-Waleed	ISBN: 9781643543420
The Islamic View of Jesus	ISBN: 9781643543352

Contents

al-Ḥāfiẓ Abū'l-Faraj 'Abdu'l-Raḥmān ibn Jawzī

His Name and Lineage

He is Abū'l-Faraj Jāmal al-Dīn 'Abḍu'l-Raḥmān ibn 'Alī ibn Muḥammad ibn 'Alī Ibn 'Ubayd Allāh Ibn al-Jawzī al-Qurashī al-Tamimi al-Bakrī from the family of Muḥammad ibn Abū Bakr *al-Ṣiddīq*, al-Baghdādī al-Ḥanbalī.[1]

His Birth and Upbringing

He was born in 509 or 510 A.H. Upon reaching adolescence, his aunt took him to Ibn Nāṣir from whom he learned a great deal. He came to love preaching while barely having reached the age of puberty, and from then started to give sermons to the people.

His father passed away when he was three years old so his aunt

[1] *Thail al-Rauḍatain*, p.21, *al-Bidāyah wa'l-Nihāyah*, p. 13/26.

took care of him. His relatives were copper merchants so at times in hadith hearings he would write his name as 'Abdu'l-Raḥmān ibn 'Alī al-Ṣaffār [i.e.The Coppersmith].

His first ḥadīth hearing was in 556 A.H., as cited by al-Dhahabi[2]

While still very young he became known as a religious person who would not socialise with anyone and would not eat from any food whose source was doubtful. He would only leave his house for prayer and he would not play with other similar to his age. He was a person of very great determination, ambition and he spent all his life busy in seeking knowledge, preaching and authoring.[3]

His Teachers

Al-Ḥāfiẓ Ibn al-Jawzī has already introduced his teachers in his book *Mashyakhat Ibn al-Jawzī* [i.e. the scholars who taught Ibn al-Jawzī] where he listed many of them. In the field of ḥadīth he benefitted from accompanying Ibn Nāṣir , in Qur'ān and *Adab* [i.e. Manners] from Sibt al-Khiyāt and Ibn al-Jawāliqī. He was the last to narrate from al-Dinawari and al-Mutawakkili.[4]

His Students

Those who narrated from him include his son and companion, the great scholar Muḥyī al-Dīn Yūsuf who was a teacher in the

[2] *Thail al-Rauḍatain*, 21, *Thail 'ala Tabaqāt al-Ḥanabila*, 1/401, *Shatharāt al-Thahab*, 4/330.

[3] *al-Bidāyah wa'l-Nihāyah*, 13/29, *Said al-Khāṭir*, 238.

[4] *Siyar al-A'lām al-Nubulā'*, 21/366, 367.

institute of al-Musta'sim billāh, his oldest son 'Alī al-Nāsikh, his grandson, the preacher Shams al-Dīn Yūsuf ibn Farghalī al-Hanafī the author of *Mir'āt al-Zamān* (Mirror of Time), al-Ḥāfiẓ 'Abd al-Ghanī, Shaykh Muwaffaq al-Dīn Ibn Qudāma, Ibn al-Dubaythī, Ibn al-Nājjar and al-Diyā.[5]

His Children

His grandson Abū al-Muẓfir and majority of those who wrote his biography say that he had three sons:

1. The oldest of them, Abū Bakr 'Abd al-'Azīz: He became a jurist in the school of Aḥmad and took knowledge from Abū al-Waqt, Ibn Nāṣir, al-Armawī and a group of his father's teachers. He traveled to the city of al-Musul where he preached and held sermons there for which he earned the people full acceptance. It is said that the family of al-Zahrazurī used to be jealous of him so they made someone poison and put it in his drink which caused him to die in al-Musul in 554 A.H. during the lifetime of his father.[6]
2. Abū al-Qāsim Badr al-Dīn 'Alī al-Nāsikh[*]
3. Abū Muḥammad Yūsuf Muḥyī al-Dīn[7]: He was the most

[5] *Siyar al-A'lām al-Nubulā'*, 21, 367.

[6] *Thail Tabaqāt al-Ḥanabila*, 1/430, 431.

[*] Publishers note: For a detail biography of him please refer to, *'The Sincere Counsel to the Students of Sacred Knowledge'*, by Ibn Jawzī, published by Dār as-Sunnah, Birmingham, UK, 2011.

[7] cf. *Siyar al-A'lām al-Nubulā'*, 23/372, *al-'Ibar*, 5/237, *Dūwal al-Islām*, 2/122, *al-Bidāyah wa'l-Nihāyah*, 13/203, *Thail Tabaqāt al-Ḥanabila*, 2/258-261, *al-'Usjud al-Masbūk*, 635, *Shatharāt al-Thahab*, 5/286287, Ibn Shaṭṭī: *Mukhtasar Tabaqāt al-Ḥanabila*, p.57.

intelligent and youngest son as he was born in 580 A.H. He became involved in preaching, he held sermons after his father, in which he excelled and by which he was looked up to by his confreres. He then was appointed to control and supervise markets of Bagdād, after that he was assigned to deliver the messages of the caliphs to kings of other different regions peculiarly to the Ayyūbī family in the Shām region. He held the position of teacher in the institute of caliph al-Mustā'sim in 640 A.H. till he was killed in prison in 656 A.H. by Hulaku who occupied Bagdād and destroyed it. His three sons Jāmal al-Dīn, Sharaf al-Dīn and Tāj al-Dīn were killed with him. He has authored many works, including *Mā'adin al-Abrīz fī Tafsīr al-Kitāb al-'Azīz* and *al-Madhab al-Aḥmad fī Madhab Aḥmad.* Unlike his brother Abu al-Qāsim, he was a dutiful son who honored his father and treated him well.

His grandson mentioned that Ibn al-Jawzī had many daughters; Rabi'a, Sharaf al-Nisā', Zainab, Jauhara, Sitt al-'Ulama al-Sughra and Sitt al-'Ulama al-Kubrā.[8]

His Uniqueness as a Preacher

Excellent indeed are the words of al-Ḥāfiẓ al-Dhahabī about him: 'He was the leading figure in reminding the people and had no equal. He would recite pleasant poetry, eloquent prose spontaneously, he spoke fine words and moving speech, which was abundant. There has never been anyone like him, not before him and not after him. He is the carrier of the flag of exhortation in its various forms. He had a pleasant appearance, a good voice and his talks had an impact on peoples' hearts. His lifestyle in general

[8] *Mir'āt al-Zamān*, 8/503, Abū Shamma: *Thail al-Rauḍatain*, 26.

was beautiful.'[9] He also said: 'I believe there will not be another one like him.'[10]

Al-Ḥāfiẓ Ibn Rajab said: 'So we conclude that his gatherings of exhortation were one of a kind and nobody had heard of anything like them. They were gatherings of great benefit where the heedless would be reminded, the ignorant would come to know, the sinners would repent and the polytheists would become Muslims.'[11]

His Works and Effects

Shaikh al-Islām Ibn Taymiyyah said in *al-Ajwiba al-Miṣriyyah*: 'Shaikh Abū'l-Faraj excelled in many sciences and has many writings to his account. He would write on many topics, I counted his works I found them to be over one thousand in number. Later, I found out about other works as well.'[12]

Having mentioned some of his books, al-Dhahabī said: 'I don't know of a scholar who has written what this man has.'[13]

The virtuous teacher 'Abd al-Ḥamīd al-'Alūjī has written a book on his works which was printed in Baghdād in 1965. In this piece he researched titles, their copies and copies that had been printed

[9] *Siyar al-A'lām al-Nubulā'*, 21/367.

[10] *Siyar al-A'lām al-Nubulā'*, 21/384.

[11] *Thail Tabaqāt al-Ḥanabila*, 1/410.

[12] *Thail Tabaqāt al-Ḥanabila*, 1/415, *al-Tāj al-Mukallal*, 70.

[13] *Tathkirat al-Ḥuffāẓ*, 1344.

and put them in alphabetic order. Whoever wishes to know about these books should refer to this work, keeping in mind that many of the manuscripts mentioned therein by al-'Alūjī have now been printed.

He authored approximately 300 books, some of his printed works include:

- *Talqīh Fuhūm Ahli al-Athār fī Mukhtasari al-Siyari wal Akhbār.*[14] [Only a portion has been printed]
- *Al-Athkiyā' wa Akhbarahum.*[15] [Printed]
- *Manāqib 'Umar ibn 'Abdul 'Azīz.*[16] [Printed]
- *Rawhu al-Arwāh.*[17] [Printed]
- *Shudhūr al-'Uqūd fī Tarikh al-'Uhūd.*[18] [Manuscript]
- *Zād al-Masīr fī 'Ilm al-Tafsīr.*[19] [Printed]
- *Al-Muntadham fī Tārikh al-Mulūk wal Umam.*[20] [Only 6 volumes have been printed]
- *Al-Dhahab al-Masbūk fī Siyaril Mulūk.*[21] [Manuscript]
- *Al-Hamqa wal Mughaffalīn.*[22] [Printed]

[14] The book mentions the historical reports concerning the Prophet (ﷺ) and his companions.

[15] A literature book in which he includes stories of intellectual people..

[16] The book details the virtues of the Caliph, 'Umar ibn 'Abdul 'Aziz.

[17] The book explains the concept of spirit and spirituality

[18] An abridged version of the known history book *Tarikh al-Mulūk wal Umam.*

[19] The book explains the science of *Tafsīr.*

[20] The book mentions the history of nations and kings.

[21] The book focuses on leaders and kings throughout history.

[22] A literature book in which he reports the stories of idiots and fools.

- *Al-Wafa fi Fada'ili al-Mustafa.*[23] [Printed]
- *Manaqib 'Umar ibn al-Khattab.*[24] [Printed]
- *Manaqib Aḥmad ibn Hanbal.*[25] [Printed]
- *Gharib al-ḥadīth.*[26] [Printed]
- *Al-Tahqīq.*[27] [Only the first volume has been printed]

And also a considerable number of works in other fields of knowledge.

The books of Ibn Jawzī available in the English language are;

1. *Ibn Jawzee's theDevils Deception* - [edited trans. Abu Ameenah Bilal Philips, Al-Hidaayah Publishing and Distribution, 1995]
2. *Disciplining the Soul* -[trans. Aymān ibn Khālid, Dār as-Sunnah Publishers, 1432/2011]
3. *Sincere Counsel to the Students of Sacred Knowledge* - [trans. Aymān ibn Khālid, Dār as-Sunnah Publishers, 1432/2011]
4. *Disturber of the Hearts* - [trans. Aymān ibn Khālid, Dār as-Sunnah Publishers, 1432/2011].

[23] The book relates the virtues of the Prophet (ﷺ).

[24] The book relates the virtues of 'Umar ibn al-Khattab.

[25] The book relates the virtues of Imam Aḥmad ibn Hanbal.

[26] The book explains one major aspect of the science of ḥadīth i.e. the ghareeb ḥadīth.

[27] The book examines the authenticity of narrations used in the known book *'al-Ta'liq al-kabir'* of al-Qadi Abū Ya'la, and how classification of ḥadīth effected scholars views.

His Death

Ibn al-Jawzī passed away on Friday the 12th of Ramaḍān in 597 A.H and was buried next to the grave of Imam Aḥmad ibn Hanbal in the cemetery of Bāb Ḥarb.[28]

[28] For a more detailed biography of al-Ḥāfiẓ Ibn al-Jawzī, refer to: Ibn Athir's *al-Kamil*, 12/71, Sibt Ibn al-Jawzī: *Mir'āt al-Zamān*, 8/481, al-Mundhirī: *al-Takmila*, Biography 608, al-Bāgghal: *al-Mashyakha*, 140, Abū Shāmma: *Thail al-Rauḍatain*, 21, Ibn al-Sā'i: *al-Jāmi'*, 9/65, Ibn Khalkān: *al-Wafayāt*, 3/140, al-Dhahabī: *al-'Ibar*, 4/297, *Dūwal al-Islām*, 2/79, *Tathkirat al-Ḥuffāẓ*, 4/1342, *Siyar al-A'lām al-Nubulā'*, 21/365, Ibn Kathīr: *al-Bidāyah wa'l-Nihāyah*, 13/26, Ibn Rajab: *Thail Tabaqāt al-Ḥanabila*, 1/399, al-Jazari: *Ghāyat wa'l-Nihāyah*, 1/375, Ṣiddīq Ḥasan Khan: *al-Tāj al-Mukallal*, 70, Ibn Shaṭṭī: *Mukhtasar Tabaqāt al-Ḥanabila*, p. 42.

Preface

Know that all that Allāh has allocated for humankind is for the purpose of benefiting them; either to bring forth a benefit such as the desire for food, or to prevent a harm such as the capability of anger. That said, when the desire for food is in excess it becomes gluttony and hence, harmful. On a similar note anger when imbalanced within a person becomes mischievous.

The purpose of this book is to employ the law of soundness and correctness through the channels of the mind and the heart, and to constrain *Hawā* so that it does not cause harm, and to treat *Hawā* that has been acted upon yet opposes the law of soundness and correctness. For this reason, I have divided this book into thirty chapters.

CHAPTER ONE

The Virtue of the Mind

PEOPLE HAVE DIFFERED REGARDING the essence of the mind and its location , subsequently this subject has been extensively discussed. In addition many ḥadīths have been narrated establishing the excellence of the mind. Some of which I have already mentioned in my book *"Dispraise of Desires"*, therefore I will not repeat them here rather I will mention a selection:

The excellence of a thing is known by its fruits, and from among the fruits of the mind is knowing the Creator, may He be exalted. For the mind has contemplated the proofs [of the existence of the Creator] until it knew Him, and has contemplated the proofs of the truthfulness of the Prophets until it recognized their truthfulness. The mind has encouraged obedience to Allāh and to His messengers. It has schemed to get all that is difficult to obtain, and it tamed the animals. It taught man to build ships on which he reached what the sea had prevented men from reaching, and tricked the birds of the sea until they were hunted. All of this while man's eyes observe the consequences and work in accordance with safety and need. Furthermore it taught man to relinquish the life of this world for the hereafter. Because of it, human beings have excellence over animals that have been prevented from having it (the mind), and it is what qualifies man for the speech of Allāh and His commandments. With it, man reaches the highest ranks that his kind can reach from the good of this world and the hereafter, in both knowledge and actions.

These virtues suffice the need to delve into detail.

CHAPTER TWO

Dispraise of *Hawā* (desires)

HAWA IS THE INCLINATION OF one's nature to what suits it and that should not be criticised when what is sought after is lawful. However, it should be dispraised when one is excessive in following *Hawā*. That said, when *Hawā* is criticised in an absolute manner, it is because most of it is either impermissible, or because people usually interpret lawfulness, and hence indulge in it in excess.

Know that part of the inner self is intellectual, the virtue of which is wisdom, the vice of which is ignorance, part of it is elicited, the virtue of which is poignancy, the vice of which is cowardice, part of it is lustful, the virtue of which is chastity and the vice of which is unrestrained *Hawā*. Exhibiting patience in the face of vice is a merit of the inner self by which a person endures both goodness and evil. Therefore, whoever lacks patience and allows his *Hawā* to lead his mind has then made the follower be followed and the led a leader. That said, it is expected that everything he desires will return to him and that he will be harmed from where he expected to benefit, he will be saddened by that which he expected happiness to come from.

Indeed human beings are favored over beastly animals with the mind (intelligence) that is designated to restrain one from following *Hawā*, therefore when a person does not accept the judgment of his mind and abides by the judgment of his *Hawā*, the beastly animal becomes better than him. From the indicative signs through which the excellence of contradicting *Hawā* is proven is the honoring and the superiority of hunting dogs over other dogs, which is due to their ability to contradict their *Hawā* and to keep what they hunt for their master out of fear of punishment or as a show of appreciation.

Know that the example of *Hawā* is like rampant flowing water leading the ship of one's nature. A person of sound mind should comprehend, enduring hardship when contradicting his *Hawā* is much easier, than enduring what comes from following it; for the least to be expected when one follows his *Hawā* is being in a state in which one neither can enjoy it nor possess the ability to prevent oneself from following it, becoming accustomed to something allows it to become an addiction; such as those addicted to sexual intercourse or alcohol.

Contemplating these matters makes it easier for a person to reject his *Hawā*. From amongst what makes *Hawā* despicable to a person is the deep reflection of oneself, upon which one will deduce that he was not created to act in conformity with his *Hawā*. For a camel eats more than he does, a bird copulates more than him, and the desires of animals are unrestricted and they do not experience regret afterwards. Thus when [knowing that] the share of humans from desires is never ultimate, and when those desires were spoiled with [human's] imperfections, accordingly humankind should know that [all these signs indicate that] they were not created to follow their own *Hawā*, notwithstanding, the dispraised

Hawā is, that which exceeds the limits and it is that which the mind judges as faulty, as I have already elucidated. Therefore whatever you desire of which there is a necessity to possess and that which assists the self to improve is praised rather than dispraised.

CHAPTER THREE

The Difference Between the Perspective of Mind and the Perspective of *Hawā*

KNOW THAT *HAWĀ* CALLS TO ATTAINING pleasure without taking into consideration its consequences, though one might know that this satisfaction will bring annoyance that actually exceeds it [exceeds the satisfaction] and also prevents one from attaining other similar satisfaction. Nonetheless *Hawā* turns one away from reflecting on all this, which makes one lower to the exact state of animals, however animals are excused because they do not observe the consequences of what they do. Hence, a wise person should not descend from a high and noble state that he is honored with, to the state of those that are low [animals], the mind should observe the consequences [of actions] one should examine the benefits and interests, since it acts as a resolute person and an advisory doctor.

The similitude of *Hawā* is that of an ignorant boy and a gluttonous sick person. For this reason, when the mind perceives something that differs to the *Hawā's* entreaty, a wise and reasonable person should then consult his mind, particularly as he is aware that it is knowledgeable as well sincere in its advice, he should be patient upon what the mind orders him to do, because knowing the excellence of the mind is enough for him to favor it. Further if he needs additional proof of the uprightness of the mind's decision, he should contemplate the consequences of following his *Hawā* such as scandalous exposure in front of people, vilification, missing virtues and good deeds. For this glory has ever deteriorated, honor has been disgraced and humiliated or a bird hunted except as a result of following *Hawā*?!

The proof can also be found when a person anticipates what his *Hawā* is calling him to prior to attaining it, he should then reflect on his state after his satisfaction has passed, he should compare this between his satisfaction and his sin for that is when he will know that he has lost double of what he has gained.

A poet said regarding this:

How much satisfaction that provoked happiness,
Ended up revealing sadness and sorrows

How many desires ripped from their participants
The garment of religion and virtue

Know that when a human acts in accordance to his *Hawā*, he will find in himself disgrace and humiliation, even if this *Hawā* does not harm him, that is because he feels subdued by his *Hawā*, but when he overcomes his *Hawā* he will find in himself honor and pride as he will feel triumphant and victorious. For this reason, when people see an ascetic they become amazed by him, and they would kiss his hand [to show respect] because they perceive him as a person who is strong enough to leave what they were weak in the face of and that is disobeying *Hawā*.

CHAPTER FOUR

Averting Passionate Love (*'Ishq*)

ISHQ IS A DISEASE THAT HAS RUINED many people whether in their bodies, religion or both; a disease for which I have composed the book *'Dispraise of Hawā'*,wherein I have listed enough cures for *'ishq*, nonetheless, I will mention some of these cures here so as not to leave out anything that this book was intended for, therefore, I say:

Whoever abstains from the amalgamation [of harmful elements causing illness] by lowering his gaze, will be saved from this disease, otherwise he will be as much diseased as he who amalgamates in such harmful acts.

If he redresses this before it becomes deeply rooted, the cure might benefit him. However if he leaves it until it becomes deeply rooted the cure will be of no benefit. Know that the mere looking at what is coveted does not result in *'ishq*, rather looking at the coveted often increases as it is aided and supported by the strength of greed, youthfulness and lust. Therefore whoever wants the cure should hasten to it before this illness becomes deeply rooted and that is by blocking the means leading to it (lowering the gaze) and by enduring it with patience. For indeed self-restraint and strength are the best of cures. The best of aids in this is fear of Allāh, restraining the disdainful self from the state of humiliation and remembering the inner flaws of the loved one. As Ibn Mas'ūd said: "If any of you like a woman, he should remember her flaws."

Whenever the loved is someone attainable and lawful to have, uniting the loved with the lover [by means of marriage] would be the best of cures. For the intensity of this disease decreases with marriage, as well as marrying more than one wife, possessing new female-slaves, travelling for long distances, thinking of the betrayal of the loved one, reading books about asceticism, remembering death, visiting the sick, and visiting cemeteries. Then one should contemplate what he wants, and how it is when he is over with it, and think of his indifference towards what he wants afterwards and how people change. Then look to the examples in himself and in others, for others might help him emerge from this chasm, and help him out of this dilemma.

I also related that a man loved a young man, then one day he looked in the mirror and noticed some grey hairs so he deserted this boy. This boy then wrote to him saying:

Why was I abandoned like never before
And the proofs of abandonment are so clear
And I see that you are drinking me, but confounding me (loving others besides him)
Although I have always known you drinking me alone (his only lover)

The man wrote back saying:

I am acting like a young-man, when in reality I am old

I am being flagged with awkwardness
Do not blame me for my disaffection
What I have wasted is enough for me
I will be held accountable for what I have done
So save me the sins I may commit
We have seen the father of mankind (Adam)
Due to a mistake, descend in humiliation (from heaven to earth)

CHAPTER FIVE

Averting Gluttony (*Sharah*)

KNOW THAT WHENEVER *Sharah* is used in a general sense it always refers to consuming food according to one's *Hawā*. There are many incidents when *Sharah* leads people to be involved in matters that lead them to harm, as it is an outcome generated from the strength of a lascivious self.

Al-Ḥārith ibn Kildah[1] said, "That which killed the animals of the wild is consuming food, after already consuming food." Others said, if the dead were asked what their reason of death was, they would say repletion."

[1] Al-Ḥārith Ibn-Kildah al-Thaqafī was the most famous medicine man in Arabia at his time and he was one of the most famous wise people of Tai'f. He travelled to Persia twice and that is where he learnt Medicine. He was born before Islām was revealed and he lived at the time of the Prophet (ﷺ) through [illegible] Jthmān, 'Alī and Mu'awiyyah. Scholars differed on whether or not he converted to Islām. The Prophet (ﷺ) used to order whoever was sick to go to him. He had words in wisdom and he wrote a book titled 'A dialogue in Medicine' based on his conversation with Kisrā Anūshruwān. *Al-'Alām* by al-Zarkali, [2:157].

It was narrated that al-Ḥasan said that Sumrah was told that his son could not sleep all night. He asked whether or not he ate a lot and they said yes. So he said, "If he dies, I will not pray the funeral prayer on him."

A man told another tauntingly, "Your father died due to excessive eating and your mother died due to excessive drinking."

'Uqbah al-Rāssibī narrated that he entered al-Ḥasan's house, whilst he was having lunch. Al-Ḥasan insisted he eat, so he told him that he was full, thereafter al-Ḥasan said, "*Subḥān Allāh*! Does a Muslim eat until he is full?!"

Section One: Excessive Eating

Know that the wise must eat to survive, on the other hand the ignorant would rather live to eat. Many a bite has prevented other bites and was the reason of death. I have elucidated the faults of satiation from food in my book *'The Picks of the Benefits'*. The intended purpose here is to constrain bingeing oneself on gluttony, so as it does not harm itself. All that I have written in the chapters that I have started this book with, namely the *'Virtue of the Mind'* and *'Dispraise of Hawā'* is more than enough to abstain from every vice and to abandon that which consequences are feared.

Section Two: Excessive Sexual Appetite

Sharah might also occur in regards to sexual intercourse. I have made it clear in my book *'The Picks of the Benefits'* that if someone indulges in it excessively his sperm channels become barred, causing unsuitable elements to enter therein and this then deprives the main organs i.e. the brain, the heart and the liver of their strength; and so sexual desire decreases and accelerates its failure. Also intercourse implies an image that honorable and estimable selves would turn away from, except if it is intended to produce children or to push away a congested evil [i.e. fear of committing adultery or fornication]. Other than that if it becomes a habit that is done for the mere sake of satisfaction and enjoyment then one is practically competing with animals.

Section Three: Hoarding Wealth

Sharah might also be in hoarding money and that is a type of 'cold insanity' if it exceeds one's needs, because money should not be sought for itself rather for spending on objects. Therefore, one who collects what he and his children need, so as not to beg off people. Gives some of it to those who are in need is not to be blamed. However a person of sound mind should not, after earning what he needs, waste his precious time and risk his priceless soul in travelling and in sailing [to collect more money]. How beautiful are the poet's words:

And he who spends days in hoarding money
For fear of poverty, then what he did is poverty itself

We have seen and heard a lot about people who are very stingy, yet travel and sail, in spite of old age, to earn money and profit - according to their claim- but they die on their travels, they do not even attain some of what they desired. This disease therefore should be treated by understanding the purpose of saving money, to balance [the risks and benefits] between earning money and risking the most precious things one possesses i.e. one's self and time. That said, whoever consults his mind will know the intended, whoever is overpowered by the disease of hoarding money will perish in the desert of greed and the only inheritor will be the mount and the packsaddle.

Section Four: Extravagance

Sharah might be in regards to pleasant arts, such as decorated buildings, fine branded horses, fancy clothes ...etc. This is a disease that originates from following *Hawā*, the cure for it is to know that the account for lawful earning is grave, extravagance is prohibited and Allāh does not look at the one who drags his garment out of pride. Allāh rewards a believer for everything except building. Therefore the wise is the one who looks at how long he is going to live, and reflects on his final abode, for that is when he will be contended with what he wears of clothes and with whatever shelters him of buildings.

It was reported that (Prophet) Nūḥ, lived in a house made of wool for nine hundred and fifty years. The Messenger (ﷺ) never put a stone over another [his house was built of mud] and on 'Umar ibn al-Khaṭṭāb's (*raḍiyAllāhu 'anhu*) garment there were twelve patches. This is because they understood that this world is a bridge and a bridge should not be taken as a home. Thus, whoever fails to be aware of this knowledge will be afflicted with the disease of *Sharah*, and should cure himself by seeking knowledge, and contemplating the biographies of the wise scholars.

CHAPTER SIX

Refusing to take a Position of Authority in this world

KNOW THAT THE INNER SELF LOVES superiority over its kind, this is why leadership is favored for the position of ordering and forbidding. Although leadership and authority is needed there are many risks in it, the least of which is discharge, the worst of which is injustice in judgement and the middle of which is wasting time if the intention of the one in charge is insincere.

A person who loves leadership and authority should know that he will think that leadership is great until he attains it. If he attains it, it becomes lowly and he will aspire to what is higher than it. For the delight disappears [after it is achieved], the sins remain [after they are committed], as well as risking oneself and one's religion. Therefore, reflecting upon all of this is the cure for the love of leadership and authority.

Abū Umāmah (*raḍiyAllāhu 'anhu*) narrated that the Prophet (ﷺ) said, "There is no man who becomes the leader of ten or what is more than that except that he will come to Allāh on the Day of

Judgment with his hand chained to his neck, his righteousness will release him or his wrongdoing will destroy him. The beginning of it [leadership] is blame, the middle of it is regret and the end of it is degradation on the Day of Judgement."[1]

Abū Hurayrah (*raḍiyAllāhu 'anhu*) narrated from the Prophet (ﷺ), that he said, "Woe to the rulers! Woe to the corporals! Woe to the ones in authority! Some people will wish that their forelocks were hanged from the Pleiades, they were swaying between the heavens and the earth rather than being responsible for anything."[2]

Imām Muslim documented in his Ṣaḥīḥ that Abū Dhar (*raḍiyAllāhu 'anhu*) said, "'Messenger of Allāh! Won't you make me responsible for anything?' So he [the Messenger] hit my shoulder with his hand and said, 'O Abū Dhar! You are weak, it is a trust, on the Day of Judgement it is a humiliation, a regret except for whoever took it rightfully and fulfilled his obligations towards it"[3]

In a different text: "O Abū Dhar! I love for you what I love for myself! Do not be the leader of two and do not be in charge of the money of an orphan."[4]

[1] Reported by al-Ṭabarānī in *al-Kabīr* [8:204], Aḥmad [5:267], Ibn-'Asākir [5:356], and Ashajari [2:226].

Al-Ḥaythami said in *Majam' al-Zawā'id* [5:204]: narrated by Aḥmad and at-Ṭabarānī. Yazīd ibn Abū Mālik is in the chain of narration, Ibn-Ḥibbān and others authenticated him and the rest of its men are reliable.

[2] Reported by Aḥmad [2:352], al-Bayhaqī [10:97] and Ibn-'Asākir [6:171].

[3] Reported by Muslim [1825].

[4] Reported by Muslim with the wording: "O Abū Dhar! I see you as weak and I love for you what I love for myself! Do not be the leader of two and do not be in charge of the money of an orphan."

CHAPTER SEVEN

Averting Stinginess

KNOW THAT WITHHOLDING MONEY is not considered stinginess as a person may wish to save for his needs, future tribulations, or for his children and relatives. This is actually considered being economical, and as such it cannot be dispraised. Further, some people may find themselves strengthened by saving their wealth. Rather the word 'stingy' is used to describe someone who does not give the obligatory rights from his wealth. Ibn 'Umar said, "Whoever gives [obligatory] alms is not stingy." Also, a person who does not give what would benefit people though doing so would not affect him or would barely affect him in any way is considered stingy.

The Prophet (ﷺ) said, "What disease is as incurable as stinginess!"[1]

Abū Muḥammad al-Rāmharmazi said, "Stinginess resembles a

[1] Reproted by al-Ḥākim in *al-Mustadrak* [3:219, 4:163-164], al-Bukhārī in *al-Adab al-Mufrad* 296, 'Abdul-Razzāq in his *Mussanaf* 20705.

disease because it spoils people, casts away honor and brings about revilement. It also weakens the body, extinguishes one's desire and changes one's color."

Wise people used to say, "A generous man is free because he owns his money, while a stingy man does not deserve to be called free because his money owns him."

'Abdullāh ibn 'Amr (*raḍiyAllāhu 'anhu*) narrated that the Prophet (ﷺ) said, "Be cautious of parsimony, for it has destroyed those who lived before you. It ordered them to sever the ties of kinship and they did, it ordered them to be stingy and they became stingy, it ordered them to indulge in dissoluteness and they did."[2]

He also said, "Two traits are not combined in a believer; stinginess and bad morals."[3]

[2] Reported by Aḥmad [2:160,195], Abū Dāwūd 1698 'Abdullāh ibn 'Umar said: The Messenger of Allāh (ﷺ) delivered a sermon in which he said, "Be cautious of miserliness, for it has destroyed those who lived before you. It has ordered them to be stingy, they became stingy, it ordered them to severe kinship ties and they did, and it ordered them to indulge in dissoluteness and they did."
Al-Khaṭṭābī said, "Miserliness is more general than stinginess, because parsimony is a hypernym and is equivalent to a genus, stinginess is a hyponym and is equivalent to a species." And most of what is said about stinginess is in individual and special cases, while miserliness is a general word and it is like a trait that is immanent, because of its inherent nature.
Some said stinginess is to withhold money while miserliness is to withhold money and kindness.
What is meant be *fujūr* (dissoluteness) here is lying. The origin of this word means to incline from truthfulness and it is said to the liar 'he has dissoluted (*fajar*) i.e. inclined from truthfulness.

[3] Reported by al-Tirmidhī 1962 and Abū Nu'aym in *al-Ḥilyah* [2:389], narrated by Abū Sa'īd al-Khudrī, May Allāh be pleased with him.

Al-Khaṭṭābī said, "Miserliness is more specific than stinginess, because miserliness is a hyponym and is equivalent to a genus while stinginess is a hypernym and is equivalent to the species."

Some said, "Stinginess is to withhold money while miserliness is to withhold money, as well as kindness."

Bishr al-Ḥāfi said, "Meeting stingy people is anguish to the hearts of the believers."

The cure for stinginess is to contemplate, as one will then realise that poor people are also one's brothers, he is favored over them [with wealth] and that they were made in need of him; therefore one should thank the One Who blessed him by consoling his brethren. One should also reflect on the honor of generosity; for people should know that you enslave free people when you do them a favor and that evil people will ravage your state when you are stingy. Such a person should be certain that everything will remain in his hands obnoxiously. Therefore it would be better to leave it before it leaves him (he should give his money in good causes, before it is taken away from him).

CHAPTER EIGHT

Prohibition on Squandering

SQUANDERING IS ONE OF THE THINGS that *Hawā* commands and the mind prohibits. The best discipline regarding this is the discipline of Allāh, Exalted is He, Who said,

وَلَا تُبَذِّرْ تَبْذِيرًا ﴿٢٦﴾

"But spend not wastefully (your wealth) in the manner of a spendthrift."

[*al-Isrā'* 17: 26]

Know that a person might be given the sustenance of one whole month in one day, but if he spends it wastefully he will suffer for the rest of the month but if he is wise, in how he spends it, he will live happily for the rest of the month.

The cure of this disease lies in reflecting on the consequences of one's actions and being cautious of the future possibility [of need] and poverty for this shall ensure the restraint of one's hand from spending wastefully.

CHAPTER NINE

Elucidation on the Amount of Earnings and Expenditure

THE EARNINGS OF A WISE PERSON should be more than what he actually needs, and he should keep some savings aside to recompense for his loss lest a misfortune occur. Further, in the event that he is unable to work and earn a living, due to some problem preventing him from doing so, his savings should be enough for him to use for the rest of his life. That said, if his wife gives birth to a child, or if he wants to marry another wife, or if he needs a servant, or if his child requires money then his earnings should suffice him. In general, expenditure should be less than earnings, so that one can set aside wealth for any misfortune that might occur, for this is what the mind; that reflects on consequences, commands, and what *Hawā*; that observes only the present state, is not concerned with.

It has been reported that Abū'l-Dardā' said, "From the deep understanding of a man is the precognition of his life."[1]

[1] Reported by Abū Nu'aym in *al-Ḥilyah* [1:211] narrated by Abū'l-Dardā' as Mawqūf.

CHAPTER TEN

Dispraise of Lying

THIS IS ONE OF THE CONTINGENCIES that *Hawā* calls to. This is because the human being, with his love of leadership and authority, prefers to be the informant and the teacher because he knows the excellence of the informant over the informed.

The cure of this disease is to know Allāh's punishment for a liar and to be certain that when a person continuously lies he will eventually be exposed one day, then he will be disrespected in such a way that cannot be averted; his shame will increase, earn people's disrespect to the extent that they will not believe him even when he is truthful, and their distrust will exceed beyond what he lied about.

'Abdullāh (*raḍiyAllāhu 'anhu*) narrated that the Messenger of Allāh (ﷺ) said, "A man keeps telling lies and endeavors in telling them until he is written a liar with Allāh." [1]

[1] Reported by Muslim in the Book *al-Birr wa'l-Ṣilah* (Virtues, Good Manners and Preserving the Ties of Kinship) ḥadīth 105.

Ibn Mas'ūd (*raḍiyAllāhu 'anhu*) said: "All traits are inherent in a believer except betrayal and lying."[2]

[2] *al-Shifā* [1:215], *al-Itḥāf* [7:518] Al-Bayhaqī weakened the *raf'* of this ḥadīth and al-Dārquṭnī said that the degree of Mawqūf is more correct.

CHAPTER ELEVEN

Averting Envy

ENVY IS TO WISH THAT THE BLESSING of the one who is envied be removed, even if the one who envies does not receive the same blessing. The reason for this disease is the love of distinction and the hatred of being equal to everyone else. This is why when someone is blessed with a grace that makes him distinct from everyone else the envious person is pained because of that distinction or because that person became equal to him. This pain will only disappear when the blessing of the one who is envied is removed. It is rare to find anyone safe from possessing some amount of envy in his heart, which is something that a person is not sinful for possessing but rather sin is only earned upon wishing for the removal of the blessings bestowed upon his Muslim brethren.

Know that envy causes insomnia, malnutrition, paleness, mood swings and continuous depression. A one hundred and twenty year old nomad was asked, "What made you live so long?" He answered, "I let go of envy, so I lived a long life."

Know that envy only occurs in regards to worldly matters as

you will not find people envying those who pray at night or those who frequently fast, neither do they envy scholars for their knowledge rather they envy those who have fame.

The cure for this disease is to know first that what Allāh has predestined will happen, trying to change what is predestined is impossible, the One who divided the sustenance between people is Judicious and Wise, He is the Possessor; He gives and He takes, for He created the universe and all that it contains.

It is as if the one who envies opposes the will of the Giver, may He be exalted. A wise man said:

'Say to the one who envies me,
'Do you know who you are misbehaving against?'
You are misbehaving against Allāh in what He gave
because you are not pleased with what He gave me
So He recompensed me for what you did and that is by
increasing me (in my blessings)
and shutting the doors of earning (a livelihood) in your face.'

Also the one who is envied did not take from the livelihood of the one who envied him nor did he take anything from his hand. Therefore, when an envier wishes someone's blessing be removed it is merely an obvious injustice.

The one who envies should look to the state of the one he envies; if what he has is from worldly matters only, then he should rightfully be pitied and not envied, because what he possesses is probably against him not for him, for the surplus of worldly matters is nothing other than trouble.

As al-Mutanabi said:

'The boy mentioned his life and his need
while the surplus of livelihood is nothing but trouble.'

The explanation of all this is; one who is rich is always afraid for his money, the one who has many slave girls is always cautious and concerned about them, a ruler is always afraid of being dismissed. Then one should know that there is depression in many favors, those favors are temporary, and that misfortunes follow them. For the possessor of a favour is always waiting for it to end or for himself to leave it. He should also be certain that envied blessings and favors are not as important and valued to the one envied, as it is to the one who envies, for people think that those who hold important positions are the happiest while, in fact, they are not aware that a person aspires to something but when he has it, he loses his interest in it for he aspires to what is higher than he possesses whilst the one who envies him still covetously views what he envies.

The one who envies therefore should know that if the one he envied punishes him, he will not be able to punish him with what is worse than what he is already suffering from. Thus, if he is not cured by any of the previous means he should work hard to attain what the one he envies has attained. One of the righteous predecessors said: "I am afraid of worries even in enviousness. For when a man envies his neighbour for being rich, he travels to do business to be as rich as his neighbour, and if he envies someone for his knowledge, he stays up all night to study. However, people have reached a point where they love idleness, and then dispraise someone who has reached a high status."

How beautiful is what al-Ridā said:

'...I am the white beautiful pure horse.
They all have their eyes on me, because
I spent the nights seeking high ranks while they slept.
If I had no respect in the eyes of others,
my enemies would have not attempted to defame me.'

Having said all that, if he who envies others cannot attain what the one he envies has attained, then he should struggle to prevent his tongue from defaming or criticising him and to confine what is in his heart.

Section One: Dispraise Envy

There are many ḥadīth that dispraise envy; Zubayr ibn al-'Awām (*raḍiyAllāhu 'anhu*) narrated that the Messenger of Allāh (ﷺ) said, "The disease of the nations before you is creeping towards you: Envy and hatred, it is the 'shaver'. I do not speak of what cuts the hair, but what severs the religion. By the One in whose hand is my soul! You will not enter paradise until you believe, and you will not believe until you love one another. Shall I tell you about something which, if you do it, you will love one another? Spread *salām* amongst yourselves."[1]

'Umar ibn Maymūn[2] said, 'Mūsā (*'alayhi as-salām*) saw a man at the throne so he envied him [i.e. liked what he saw so he wished it

[1] Reported by Aḥmad [1:165,167], al-Bayhaqi [10:232], al-Baghawi in *Sharḥ-u-Sunnah* [12:259] and at-Tirmidhi 2510.

[2] 'Umar Ibn-Maymūn; al-Ḥāfiẓ said in *at-Taqrīb*: He is Ibn-Baḥr Ibn-Sa'd Ibn-u-Rammāḥ al-Balkhī Abū 'Alī al-Qāḍī he is reliable and was blinded. He is from the seventh level. Tirmidhī reported from him.

for himself, without wishing that the blessing be taken away from the man] and asked people about him. They said, 'Do you want to know about his deeds?' 'He does not envy people for what Allāh bestowed upon them of His grace, he does not walk about spreading malicious gossip and he is not disobedient to his parents.'

Salim narrated from his father (*raḍiyAllāhu 'anhu*) that the Messenger of Allāh (ﷺ) said "Envy is not justified except in the case of two individuals only: one who Allāh has blessed with the Qur'ān, so he prays reciting it during the night and day. And a man who Allāh gave wealth, so he spends it rightfully during the night and the day."[3]

[3] Agreed upon, reported by al-Bukhārī [2:134, 9:78, 126], Muslim [p.559].

CHAPTER TWELVE

Averting Spitefulness

SPITEFULNESS IS THE TRACES remaining of others unpleasant actions and words, in the inner self, of the one was spited. For indeed, the mind decides the traces of others unpleasant deeds to remain as it decides for the traces of others pleasant deeds to remain.

'Abdullāh ibn Ka'b ibn Malik narrated that he heard Ka'b ibn-Malik's story when he did not join the Messenger of Allāh (ﷺ) in Tabūk and the story of the revelation of the acceptance of his repentance. He said, "I entered the Masjid, while the people were gathered around the Messenger of Allāh (ﷺ), so Ṭalḥah ibn 'Ubaydillah ran to me, shook my hand and congratulated me. By Allāh! He was the only man of the immigrants who did that." He said, "So Ka'b never forgot Ṭalḥah for this."[1]

So if it is proven that good deeds and favors are not forgotten, so too are bad deeds not forgotten. Nevertheless it is preferred to try and remove the traces of any ugly deed from the heart. The

[1] Reported by al-Bukhārī [6:4] and Muslim [53].

cure of spitefulness is forgiveness and remission.

There are two stages of forgiveness: First is to know the reward of someone who forgives, second to thank the One Who made one be in the position of the forgiver and the other in the position of one who errs. The perfection of forgiveness can be reached through being content and this happens by removing all that is in the heart against the other person.

There is a more precise cure than this that I have mentioned and it is that a person knows that he was harmed because of a sin that he committed, or to wipe away a sin, or to raise his rank, or to test his patience. Yet a more precise cure is to understand that everything that happens to him is from the One who predestines.

CHAPTER THIRTEEN

Averting Anger

I HAVE MADE IT CLEAR THAT ANGER is placed in the nature of a human being so as to keep harm away from him and so that he can take revenge from the one who harms him. However, what is detested is excessive anger, as it disturbs one's soundness, makes one imbalanced and immoderate, such a person starts making wrong decisions which may even affect he who is angry more than the person he is angry at.

Anger is heat that spreads when something provokes one's anger, it makes the blood of desire boil to take revenge, and may even cause a fever. The main reason for anger is usually arrogance, for a person is never angry at anyone who is higher than him. That said, the cure for this is that the angry person changes his state; if he is talking he should be silent, if he is standing he should sit, and if he is sitting he should lie down, so that he may calm down. If he leaves the place immediately and leaves the one he is angry at, it would be better. He should also reflect on the excellence of repressing anger, for Allāh has praised those who repress anger, He said,

وَٱلْكَـٰظِمِينَ ٱلْغَيْظَ وَٱلْعَافِينَ عَنِ ٱلنَّاسِ

"Those who repress anger and forgive other people"
[*Āli 'Imrān* 3:134]

And if he reflects on the fact that this might be happening to him because of a sin that he committed or that it is all predestined then the matter will become easier for him, just as I mentioned in the previous chapter.

Section One: Ḥadīth regarding Anger

There are many ḥadīth that were narrated regarding anger. Abū Huryarah (*raḍiyAllāhu 'anhu*) said, "A man came to the Prophet (ﷺ) and said, 'Advise me!' He said, 'Do not get angry!' The man kept repeating his request and the Prophet (ﷺ) continued to reply, 'Do not get angry!'"[1]

The Messenger (ﷺ) said, "The strong is not the one overcomes the people by his strength, but the strong is the one who controls himself while in anger."[2]

Bukhārī and Muslim also reported that Sulayman ibn Sard (*raḍiyAllāhu 'anhu*) said, "I was sitting with the Prophet (ﷺ) and two men were cursing each other, the face of one of them was red and swollen (because of his anger). Thereafter the Prophet (ﷺ) said, 'I know a word which if he says, what he feels will be gone. If he says 'I seek refuge in Allāh from the damned devil' What he feels will be gone." So they said, "The Prophet (ﷺ) said,

[1] Reported by al-Bukhārī [8:35].

[2] Reported by al-Bukhāri [8:34] and Muslim [2014].

'We seek refuge in Allāh from the damned devil!' He said, 'Am I crazy?!'"

Abū Dāwūd reported in his Sunan from the ḥadīth of Abū Dhar (*raḍiyAllāhu 'anhu*) that the Prophet (ﷺ) said, "If any of you gets angry while standing, let him sit down. If his anger does not go away, then he should lie down."[3]

Al-Khaṭṭābī said, "The one who is standing is ready to make any movement, to hurt anyone and the one who is sitting is less likely to do anything."

Ibn 'Abbās (*raḍiyAllāhu 'anhu*) narrated that the Prophet (ﷺ) said, "If any one of you becomes angry, he should be quiet."

Al-Aḥnaf said, "Anything that prevents one from controlling one's temper while angry is the devil of hastiness."

Section Two: Excessive Anger

If an angry person does not become calm when his anger peaks, he may harm himself or the person he is angry at and he would certainly regret any actions he may take afterwards. Many people have killed, hurt, and broken bones for their children while they were angry and regretted what they did for the rest of their lives. Some actually harmed themselves; a man was very angry at one time so he screamed, his blood expectorated instantly and he died

[3] Reported by Abū Dāwūd in *al-Adab*, chapter 4 [4782], Aḥmad [5:152], *Sharḥ-us-Sunnah* [3:162], *Mawārid al-Aẓmān* 1973. Al-Baghawī said, "He ordered him to sit down and lie down, so as he does not do, while he is angry, what he will regret afterwards. That is because someone who is lying down is less likely to move or to hurt anyone compared to someone who is sitting or standing."

at once. Another angry man punched someone due to his anger and his fingers broke, absolutely nothing happened to the one he punched.

To cure this disease one should envisage what he looks like when he is angry and what he looks like when he is calm. This is when he will know that anger is a state of insanity and immoderation. If the angry person does not change his mind about hitting the one he is angry at but he promises himself to do so but first to change his state (sit down if he is standing etc). If he does that then he will see the ugliness of what he was about to do and therefore he will leave it.

Section Three: The Excellence of Repressing Anger

When our righteous predecessors used to become angry, they would forgive, seeking the excellence of repressing anger. Some of them believed that they were angered because of their sins, and some believed that they were being tested, yet others believed that they were angered for other reasons that I have previously mentioned in the chapter on spitefulness.

It was mentioned in some of the previous revealed books of Allāh, that Allāh said: "O son of Adam! Remember Me when you are angry, I will remember you when you sin so that I will not destroy you with those I destroy. If you were wronged, be content with My support for My support is better for you than your own victory for yourself."

Mawriq said, "I have never said a word, when angry that I have regretted, when I am calm,"

And Ibn 'Awn was never angry. When a man would make him angry, he would say, 'May Allāh bless you!"

Section Four: Being Composed before Reprimanding

A person who is angry at another should not punish him while he is angry, that is if he deserves to be punished at all. He should rather wait until he calms down, so that his punishment is equal to the offense not equal to his anger.

A man was brought to 'Umar ibn 'Abdul 'Azīz, who 'Umar was angry at. He told him, "If I was not angry at you, I would have beaten you." And then he let him go.

CHAPTER FOURTEEN

Averting Arrogance

ARROGANCE IS GLORIFYING one's self and disdaining others. The reason why arrogance occurs is due to feeling superior over others that are less in lineage, wealth, knowledge, or worship etc. The sign of arrogance is disdaining those who one feels superior over, also swaggering, pride and one's love for being glorified by others.

The cure for this disease lies in two approaches: a general approach and a detailed approach. The general approach is further divided into two types; theoretical and practical. The theoretical cure is through textual and logical evidence of the demerits of arrogance. The practical cure is achieved by accompanying humble people and hearing their stories.

On the other hand the detailed approach is achieved by reflecting on the flaws of the self and knowing that if someone is proud about his money, it will soon be taken away from him. He should also know that excellence lies in being sufficient from a thing, not in needing it. If it is knowledge that he is proud about, then he should know that many people, who are more knowledgeable than him, and preceded him in that path. Moreover his knowledge forbids him from arrogance, so it is an evidence against him. In addition if it is a deed that is making him proud, then looking at it and thinking that it is perfect is a demerit not a merit.

Section One: Arrogance in the Heart

Abū Salamah narrated that 'Abdullāh ibn 'Amr (*raḍiyAllāhu 'anhuma*) ran across ibn 'Umar (*raḍiyAllāhu 'anhuma*) on the hill of Marwah, so they descended and talked. And then 'Abdullāh ibn 'Amr left and ibn 'Umar sat and wept. He was asked, "Why are you weeping?" He said, "He ('Abdullāh ibn 'Amr) claims that he heard the Messenger of Allāh (ﷺ) say, 'Whoever has an atom's weight of arrogance in his heart, Allāh will throw him in the hellfire on his face.'"[1]

Iyās ibn Salamah (*raḍiyAllāhu 'anhu*) reported that his father said, "The Messenger of Allāh (ﷺ) said, "A man shall glorify himself until he is written among the tyrants, so that he suffers from what befell them."[2]

Muslim reported that Ibn Mas'ūd (*raḍiyAllāhu 'anhu*) narrated from the Prophet (ﷺ) that he said, "Whoever has an atom's weight of arrogance in his heart will not enter paradise." A Man said, "A man likes that his garment is nice and that his shoes are nice." He (ﷺ) also said, "Indeed Allāh is Beautiful and He loves beauty.

[1] Reported by al-Bayhaqī [10:191]. Al-Haythamī, referred it in *'Majma' az-Zawā'id'* to al-Ṭabarānī in *al-Kabir* and Aḥmad. Al-Haythamī said: Its men are in the ṣaḥīḥ (Bukhārī and Muslim reported a ḥadīth from these men in their Ṣaḥīḥs)

[2] Reported by at-Tirmidhī 2000, al-Baghawī in *Sharḥ-us-Sunnah* [13:167] and al-Daylamī 7576. 'Umar Ibn-Rashid is in the chain of narration, he is weak.

Arrogance is rejecting the truth and disdaining people."[3]

Muslim reported from al-Aghar from Abū Hurayrah (*raḍiyAllāhu 'anhu*) and Abū Sa'īd (*raḍiyAllāhu 'anhu*) that they narrated that the Messenger of Allāh (ﷺ) said, "Allāh, glorified and exalted is He, says: 'Pride is my cloak, and glory is my lower garment, so whoever contends with Me regarding either one of them, I will torment him."

Al-Khaṭṭābī said, "This means that pride and greatness are two attributes of Allāh that He alone is particularised with, no one shares them with Him, no created being should have them because the attribute of the created is humbleness and lowness. Allāh has set the cloak and the lower garment as an example; no one shares his cloak, or his lower garment with another person. Likewise Allāh does not share his pride and greatness with anyone, and Allāh only knows."

He (al-Khaṭṭābī) said, "And his saying: 'Whoever has an atom's weight of arrogance in his heart will not enter paradise,' may have two meanings: the first is that this refers to the arrogance of disbelief and the second is that He takes arrogance out of the hearts of those who will enter paradise. And his saying: 'disdaining people' means looking down at them and belittling them."

Al-Ḥasan said, "You see people praising a man extravagantly, saying to him, you are indeed such and such, so he just sits silently believing what is being said to him, and you see a man walking

[3] Reported by Muslim in the Book *al-Birr wa'l-Ṣilah* (Virtues, Good Manners and Preserving the Ties of Kinship) ḥadīth 136 under the text 'Glory is His lower garment and pride is His cloak, so whoever contends with me, I will torment him.'

slowly and boastfully, not in a normal manner [he does that out of arrogance].”

CHAPTER FIFTEEN

Averting Conceit

CONCEIT ORIGINATES FROM LOVING the self. For indeed the faults of the beloved are never noticed and are not believed to be flawed, rather they are seen as perfect, by the lover.

From among the consequences of conceit is that it leads to detesting the thing that caused conceit in the first place, because the one who possesses conceit regarding a matter does not increase himself in it, rather he advances to find faults in others.

The cure for conceit is to know one's faults, as I have mentioned earlier, to ask other people about one's flaws, to reflect on the state of those who preceded him and had what he has [i.e. conceit]. Therefore, when a scholar has conceit regarding his knowledge he should read the biographies of scholars who preceded him, or when one has conceit regarding his asceticism, then he should read the biographies of ascetics. For this is when he shall not be proud of himself. [How can a person have self-conceit when knowing that] Imam Aḥmad knew one million ḥadīth by heart, and Kahmas ibn al-Ḥasan used to recite the whole Qur'ān three times a day, and Salmān al-Taymī prayed Fajr with the same *wūḍū'* (ablution) of *Ishā'* for forty years.

Whoever reflects on the lives of other people would know that he, compared to them, is like a man who has a dinar, he is so happy with it, yet he does not know that there are people who have thousands and thousands of dinars.

Ibrāhīm al-Khawās said, "Conceit prevents from knowing one's capabilities and limits."

A wise man said, "A man's conceit of himself is an enemy of his mental capacities, and how harmful is conceit to the merits."

CHAPTER SIXTEEN

Averting *Riyā'* (Insincerity and Pretentiousness)

WHOEVER KNOWS ALLĀH TRULY will make all his deeds sincere to Him. For *riyā'* occurs when someone lacks knowledge of His Creator, when he does not glorify Allāh as should be, when the inner self seeks people's compliments and praise.

People vary in this disease, some seek praise from others only, some seek [the pleasure of] Allāh in their deeds as well as people's praise, some do not seek people's praise at all, however when people see them doing good deeds, they improve their work to be praised. In the latter case it becomes a lesion that has affected a good deed.

The general cure for this disease is to know Allāh truly. For whoever knows Him would make all his actions sincerely for Him and would not see anyone besides Him. He would locate himself in the position of the worshipper, who is humble to his Worshipped God, not in the position of the praised worshipped God. He would know that reward is given only for sincere deeds, therefore he should be aware of the wasted exhaustion (of performing acts for other than the sake of Allāh).

Moreover he should know that punishment for *riyā'* is severe. 'Umar ibn al-Khaṭṭāb (*raḍiyAllāhu 'anhu*) narrated that the Prophet (ﷺ) said, "Deeds are considered by their intention, and a person will be rewarded according to his intention."[1]

Abū Mūsā (*raḍiyAllāhu 'anhu*) narrated that a man came to the Prophet (ﷺ) and said, "O Messenger of Allāh! Tell me if a man fights in the battlefield out of valor, out of zeal, and out of hypocrisy, which of these is considered fighting in the cause of Allāh?" The Messenger said, "He who fights in order that the word of Allāh reigns supreme, is considered as fighting in the cause of Allāh." [2]

It was narrated from Abū Hurayrah (*raḍiyAllāhu 'anhu*) that Nāṭil Ashāmī said, "O Shaykh! Relate to us a ḥadīth that you have heard from the Messenger of Allāh (ﷺ)." Abū Hurayrah (*raḍiyAllāhu 'anhu*) said, "I heard the Messenger of Allāh (ﷺ) say, 'The first to be judged on the Day of Judgement will be a man who died as a martyr. He shall be brought forth. Allāh will make him recount His blessings (i.e. the blessings which He had bestowed upon him) and he will recount them (and admit having enjoyed them in his life). (Then) Allāh will say: What did you do (to requite these blessings)? He will say: I fought for you until I died as a martyr. Allāh will say: You have told a lie. You fought that you might be called

[1] Agreed upon. Reported by al-Bukhārī [1:2, 8:175, 9:29] and Muslim in the Book of *Imarāh* ḥadīth 155.

[2] Agreed upon. Reported by al-Bukhārī [1:43, 4:25,105, 9:166] and Muslim in the Book of *Imarāh* ḥadīth 149-150 and 151.

"a brave warrior". And you were called so. (Then) orders will be passed against him and he will be dragged with his face downward and cast into Hell. Then will be brought forward a man who acquired knowledge, who imparted it (to others) and recited the Qur'ān. He will be brought, Allāh will make him recount His blessings, he will recount them (and admit having enjoyed them in his lifetime). Then Allāh will ask: What did you do (to requite these blessings)? He will say: I acquired knowledge and disseminated it and recited the Qur'ān seeking your pleasure. Allāh will say: You have told a lie. You acquired knowledge so that you might be called 'a scholar' and you recited the Qur'ān so that it might be said: 'He is a reciter' and such has been said. Then orders will be passed against him, he shall be dragged with his face downward and cast into the Fire. Then will be brought a man whom Allāh had made abundantly rich and had granted every kind of wealth. He will be brought, Allāh will make him recount His blessings, he will recount them (and admit having enjoyed them in his lifetime). Allāh will (then) ask: What have you done (to requite these blessings)? He will say: I spent money in every cause in which you wished that it should be spent. Allāh will say: You are lying. You did (so) that it might be said about (You): 'He is generous' and so it was said. Then Allāh will pass orders, he will be dragged with his face downward and thrown into Hell." [3]

[3] Reported by Muslim in the Book of *Imarāh* ḥadīth 152.

He was mentioned as 'Qa'il Ashāmī' however it is a typing error and the correct name is 'Nātil Ashamī'. An-Nawawī said in his explanation of Ṣaḥīḥ Muslim [4:568], "He is Nātil ibn Qays al-Ḥāzimī Ashāmī from Palestine. His father was a companion and Nātil was the head of his clan."

Al-Nawawī said in his explanation of this ḥadīth the generalities that are mentioned in regards to the excellence of *Jihad* is for the one who is sincere in it, as well as the praise of scholars and those who spend money for the sake of Allāh in charity is attributed to those who do that sincerely for Allāh's sake.

Abū Hurayrah (*raḍiyAllāhu 'anhu*) narrated that the Prophet (ﷺ) narrated from his Lord that He said, "I am the best of partners, so whoever does an act of worship, committing *shirk* in it, I am free from him, and he is left to the partner he associated Me with."[4]

Maḥmūd ibn Lubayd (*raḍiyAllāhu 'anhu*) narrated that the Messenger of Allāh (ﷺ) said, "What I fear for you the most is minor *Shirk*!' They said, 'O Messenger of Allāh! What is that?' He said, '*Riyā*'. Allāh, Exalted is He, says on the Day of Judgement, after he recompenses people for their deeds: Go to those who you used to show your deeds off to and see if they have a recompense."[5]

Abū Ḥāzim said, "No servant (of Allāh) betters what is between him and other servants, and he does not spoil what is between him and Allāh, except that Allāh spoils what is between him and the servants of Allāh. Working for the sake of one face is easier than working for the sake of all faces. For if you work for the sake of that face (the face of Allāh), all faces will turn to you but if you spoil it, all faces will detest you."[6]

[4] Reported by Muslim in the Book of *Zuhd* (Asceticism) ḥadīth 46, Aḥmad [2:301], Ibn Khuzaymah 938, Ibn Majah in the Book of *Zuhd* 21.

[5] Reported by Aḥmad [5:428].

[6] Reported by Abū Nu'aym in *al-Ḥilyah* [3:239]. Through the chain of Aḥmad Ibn Ḥanbal from 'Alī ibn 'Ayāsh from Muḥammad ibn Maṭraf from Abū Ḥāzim, he said, "No servant (of Allāh) amends what is between him and Allāh, except that Allāh amends what is between him and other servants. And he does not spoil what is between him and Allāh, except that Allāh spoils what is between him and the servants of Allāh.Blandishing one face is easier than blandishing all faces. For if you blandish that face (the face of Allāh), all faces will turn to you and if you spoil it all faces will detest you.

Ibn Tawbah Abū Ja'far 'Abdullāh said, "I saw Abū Bakr al-Adamī, the reciter, in a dream after his death, begging. I told him, 'What did Allāh do with you?' He said, 'I have stood in front of Him and I have suffered many tribulations.' So I told him, 'What about the nights, the good deeds, and the Qur'ān?!' He said, 'There was nothing that was worse for me than them because I did them all for [the sake of] *dunya*!' I said, 'So what happened to you?' He said, 'Allāh, May He be exalted, told me, 'I took it upon myself not to torture anyone who reached eighty years of age.'"

CHAPTER SEVENTEEN

Averting Excessive Thinking

KNOW THAT THINKING IS NEEDED to remember what was forgotten, and to think about future benefits. However if thinking is about that which is not fruitful it will be harmful, and if it is excessive it will exhaust the body.

The hypocrites say, "Scholars should leave thinking for some time, lest they exhaust their bodies." I said, a wise person should not stop thinking about what he can attain. However when a layman thinks of becoming the Caliph, that he is as knowledgeable as Abū Hanīfah or Al-Shāfiʿī, that he is an ascetic exactly like Bishr al-Hafi and Maʿrūf al-Karkhī, to have the wealth of ʿAbdul Raḥmān ibn ʿAwf, these thoughts exhaust the body, especially if he is only thinking and is idle (instead of working hard to achieve what he wants). A person should rather think about that which is possible for him to achieve, and what he can attain from good deeds. He should also think about his struggle against evil. For many sinners reflected on their consequences and repented, many kings reflected on the vanity of this life, to became ascetic.

Ibn 'Abbās (*raḍiyAllāhu 'anhuma*) said, "Praying two rak'at with contemplation is better than praying all night while the heart is heedless."[1]

Umm al-Dardā' (*raḍiyAllāhu 'anha*) was asked, "What was the best deed of Abū'l-Dardā'?" She said, "Contemplation and thoughtfulness."[2]

Mālik ibn Dinār stood on his feet praying until dawn and said, "The people of the hellfire, in their chains and iron collars, kept presenting to me until dawn."

Some wise men used to say, "Warding off thinking brings blindness."

[1] Reported by Ibn ul-Mubārak in the Book of *Zuhd* p.403, and Muḥammad ibn Naṣr in the Book of *Qiyām-ul-Layl* p.60.

[2] Reported by Ibn ul-Mubārak in the Book of *Zuhd* p.302 through the chain of 'Awn ibn 'Abdullāh from Umm al-Dardā' that he was asked, "What was the most frequent act of Abū'l-Dardā'?" She said, "Contemplation."

Reported by Abū Nu'aym in *al-Ḥilyah* [1:208] "She said, 'Contemplation and thoughtfulness." [1:209] Abū'l-Dardā' said, "Contemplating for an hour is better than praying one whole night."

CHAPTER EIGHTEEN

Averting Excessive Sadness

KNOW THAT (THE HEART OF) a person of sound mind cannot be free of sadness, because he remembers his previous sins, therefore becomes saddened, he thinks about his negligence, reflects on what the scholars and the righteous have said, as a result he becomes sad for not taking heed.

Mālik ibn Dinār said, "If a heart is devoid of sadness, it will become desolate. Just as a house becomes desolate if no one resides in it."[1]

Ibrāhīm ibn ʿĪsā[2] said, "I have not seen a person with as much sadness as al-Hasan; whenever I see him, I assume that he has just

[1] Reported by Abū Nuʿaym in *al-Ḥilyah* [2:360] from Mālik ibn-Dinār he said, "If there is no sorrow in the heart, it will desolate, just like a house desolates if there is no resident in it."

. Abū Nuʿaym said, "Ibrāhīm ibn Īsā, the ascetic, he accompanied Maʿrūf al-Karkhī and heard form Abū Dāwūd at-Tayālisī and Muhammad ibn al-Muqrīʾ."

recently been afflicted with a trial."

Mālik ibn Dinār said, "As much as you grieve for this world, the fear of the Day of Judgement leaves your heart." Thus, as it is evident that sadness accompanies the heart of the righteous, excessive sadness therefore should be avoided. That is because one should feel sad regarding what he has missed, and I have already clarified the way to recant.

It was mentioned in a ḥadīth, "The rest of the life of a believer is invaluable, he can recant in it what he has missed." If sadness is related to something that cannot be recanted then it is of no use, however if it is related to a religious matter then he should make it up with the aid of hoping for the Graciousness and Mercifulness of Allāh. On the other hand if one has sadness in regards to worldly matters and whatever he misses from it, then that is an evident loss, a wise person should rid himself of that.

The best of the cures for sadness is to know that one cannot bring back what he has missed, rather by feeling sad he is adding another misfortune to the already existing misfortune ultimately making two misfortunes. Also a misfortune should not be made heavier by being saddened by it, rather it should be eased and pushed away. Ibn 'Amr said, "If Allāh takes something away from you, get busy with anything that will not make you think about it." In addition, what Allāh gives you instead of what was taken away from you makes that easier. However, if there is nothing that can make the matter easier, then one should struggle to push away sadness from his heart.

Know that what calls to sorrow and sadness is *Hawā* not the mind, simply because the mind does not call to that which is not useful. One should know that the matter, eventually, will get easier after some time, therefore he should strive to bring forward that which is supposed to happen then (i.e. comfort) so that he relaxes during the time of difficulty until such ease and comfort is achieved. One of the things that make sorrow and sadness disappear is knowing that it is useless, believing in its reward and remembering those who are afflicted with worse misfortunes.

CHAPTER NINETEEN

Averting *Ghamm* (Grief) and *Hamm* (Worry)

GHAMM OCCURS DUE TO MISFORTUNES that happened in the past while *hamm* occurs due to an expected misfortune in the future. When someone has the feeling of grief in regard to his past sins, his grief will benefit him, because he is rewarded for it. Whoever worries about a good deed he wishes to do, his worry will benefit him as well. However if someone grieves for something that he missed from this world, then [he should know] that the missed thing will not return and that grief harms, so practically he is adding harm to harm, as I have mentioned in the previous chapter.

A resolute person should protect himself from what brings about grief, and that is losing an object he loves. Therefore, whoever has many objects that he loves, his grief increases, and whoever decreases his objects of love his grief decreases accordingly. Someone may say, when I have no objects of love I also still have grief, we affirm this but we say to him; your grief over not having a loved one is not even a tenth of the grief experienced by the one who has lost a loved one. Have you not noticed that the one who does not have a child lives in grief but not as much as the one who lost his child?! Moreover when a person becomes accustomed to what he loves and enjoys it for a long period of time, it takes over his heart, therefore when he loses it he will feel the bitterness of his loss which will be greater than all the satisfaction he had during his lifetime. This is because the loved one is corresponding to the self just as health corresponds to it, which causes the self not to find satisfaction except in it, for its absence disturbs it. This is why the self grieves for its loss much more than it rejoices in its presence, because the inner self believes that what it had was its given right to possess. Therefore a wise person should monitor the closeness between himself, his beloved to ensure it remains moderately balanced, however if he requires that which brings about grief [i.e. loving some object or person], this causes grief then the cure is first to believe in predestination and that whatever Allāh predestines is going to happen. He should then know that life is founded on distress, all constructed buildings shall eventually be ruined, all gatherings shall eventually depart, and whoever wants the lasting of what does not last is like he who wants what does not exist to exist. Therefore he should not ask of life what it was not created for.

A poet said:

> It [worldly life] is founded on distress yet you want it,
> Free of harm and distress

One should imagine that what befell him is multiplied, for this is when what he suffers will be easier on him. It is a habit of smart porters to put something heavy on top of what they are carrying, and then after taking a few steps, to remove the heavy object as that makes what they are carrying feel lighter.

One should also wait, in times of prosperity for an attack of tribulation, so that if any tribulation befalls him, he should think of what remains instead of what he has lost so that when part of that befalls him it becomes very easy on him. Such as when someone loses some money so he counts what remains, and then considers the remaining as a profit. Or if someone imagines that he loses his eyesight, so that when he has ophthalmia, it becomes easy on him to bear this illness, likewise with the rest of harmful matters.

A poet said:

The prudent imagines in himself,
his tribulations before they befall him.
If they suddenly befall him,
they do not surprise him because he had already imagined them.
And the ignorant trusts the days,
and he forgets the demise of those who came before him.
So when trials of times surprise him,
with some trials he becomes lost.
Though if he was strict in his affairs,
patience would have taught him boldness

A member of the righteous predecessors said, "I saw a woman, whose youthfulness surprised me, I said, '[There is no doubt] This face has never suffered from sorrow or sadness.' She said, 'Do not say that! For I do not know anyone who has suffered from what I have suffered. I had a husband who bought a sacrificial animal and slaughtered it, and we had two sons. The eldest told the one younger than him, 'Come and I will show you how our father slaughtered the ewe.' So he slaughtered his brother. When we started to look for him, he ran away and my husband died while looking for him.' I said, 'So how are you handling your sorrow?' She said, 'If I could find aid in sorrow I would have employed it.'

Section One: Treating Sorrow, Sadness and Grief

Sorrow, sadness and grief may befall one due the prevalence of blackness, which should be treated with what will remove this blackness; which are the things that bring about joy. Grief freezes the blood while happiness heats it until its intrinsic heat is raised, both of them (happiness and grief) can harm, and may lead to death, if they are not immediately kept within moderate levels.

CHAPTER TWENTY

Averting Excessive Fear and Cautiousness of Death

FEAR AND CAUTIOUSNESS OCCUR in matters related to the future. A resolute person is he who prepares for what he fears before it befalls him, and avoids excessive fear of what must inevitably befall him, because (in this case) his fear does not benefit him. Indeed the fear of Allāh was so intensified in the hearts of many righteous people that they asked Allāh to decrease it. The reason behind asking Allāh such is that fear is like a lash; if a camel is lashed continuously it will worry, but the lash should be used when it is lazy in order to motivate it.

It was narrated that Sufyān al-Thawrī told a young man who was sitting with him, "Do you want to fear Allāh truly and rightfully?" The young man said, "Yes." Sufyān said, "You are a fool! If you fear Him truly you would not be able to fulfill the obligatory acts!"[1]

[1] Sufyān al-Thawrī: ibn Sa'īd ibn Masrūq, Abū 'Abdullāh al-Thawrī, one of the great *imams* and worshippers of this nation. He was titled 'The Leader of Believers in Ḥadīth' and was well versed in *tafsīr*. He was the teacher of Abū Ḥanīfah and Mālik amongst others and died in the year 161H.

Section One: Excessive Fear

A person of sound mind should not fear illness excessively, because it must inevitably befall him some time during his life and fearing what is inevitable is merely an increase in harm. As for fearing death and thinking about it, it is something that is hard to do but what eases it, is knowing that death is inevitable so caution does not benefit the person in anyway rather it increases one's cautiousness. Every time a person imagines the intensity of death, he experiences it emotionally, this is why he should not picture death in his mind, he will only die once, not multiple times, and avoiding thinking about it will ease it.

A person should also know that Allāh is able to make it easier, if He Wills, and that what is after death is more disturbing than death itself, because death is a bridge that takes us to our eternal dwelling. However, one should frequently think about death to work towards it, not just for the sake of imagination.

If the thought of leaving this life saddens the heart, then the cure is to know that this world is not a dwelling of satisfaction, rather its pleasure and satisfaction is in departing it, therefore this is not something that one should compete to possess. Thus, a wise person is saddened by leaving this life only because of the righteous deeds he will miss performing, and that is why the righteous predecessors used to be saddened by death as well. When Mu'adh ibn Jabal was on his death bed, he said, "O Allāh! You know that I did not love this world and living long in it for the beauty of flowing rivers or for planting trees. Rather for fasting hot days, forbearing in acts of worship for hours and joining scholars in circles of Your remembrance."

Section Two: Curing the Whispers

When death befalls someone, he should know that it is an hour of serious suffering because it is a moment of severe pain, when he is leaving all objects of love, his loved ones, add to all that the horror of the throes of death and fear of where his wealth will go. Then *Shayṭān* comes and attempts to have the slave [of Allāh] become discontent with his Lord, he tells him, 'Look at you! What made you die? Is it painful? You are leaving your wife, your children and you will be laid under the ground!' So he might cause him to become discontent with his Lord, hating Allāh's decree, making him say things that include any kind of objection, or he might make him unjust in his will, giving some of the inheritors preference over others, so on and so forth. In this case, we need to cure the whispers of *Shayṭān* and cure the self.

Abū Dāwūd reported from Abū al-Yusr (*raḍiyAllāhu 'anhu*) that the Prophet (ﷺ) used to say,

« أعوذ بك أن يتخبطني الشيطان عند الموت »

"I seek refuge in You that *Shayṭān* flounders me at death."[2]

[2] Reported by Abū Dāwūd 1552-1553, al-Nasa'ī [8:283] through the chain of Afla' Mawlā (emancipated slave) of Abū Ayyūb from Abū al-Yusr that the Prophet (ﷺ) used to pray, "O Allāh! I seek refuge in you from dying under abolishment, not being deliberate, I seek refuge in you from drowning, from burning and from senility, I seek refuge in you that *Shayṭān* flounders me at death, I seek refuge in you that I die while escaping from fighting for Your sake and I seek refuge in you from dying because of a sting."

Al-Khaṭṭāb said, "His seeking refuge in the 'floundering of *Shayṭān* at death', that is if *Shayṭān* seizes him when he leaves this world, preventing him from repenting or hinders him from mending his affairs, leaving an injustice or he makes him despair from the mercy of Allāh or makes him hate death or be =

In that minute *Shayṭān* tells his assistants, "If you miss him now [i.e. you do not succeed to lead him astray before he dies], you will never catch him again [i.e. you will never be able to deviate him at any other time]." As for the cure for these trials we should first mention that whoever is mindful of Allāh while in good health, Allāh will protect him when he is ill, and whoever observes Allāh in his thoughts, Allāh will protect him when he moves his bodily parts.

Ibn 'Abbās (*raḍiyAllāhu 'anhu*) narrated from the Prophet (ﷺ) that he said, "Be mindful of Allāh and He will protect you. Be mindful of Allāh and you will find Him before you. Know Him while in prosperity, He will know you in distress."[3]

You have known the story of Prophet Yūnus (Jonah) - when he had previous righteous deeds that enabled his release him from the trial he suffered. Allāh, May He be exalted, said,

فَلَوْلَآ أَنَّهُۥ
كَانَ مِنَ ٱلْمُسَبِّحِينَ ﴿١٤٣﴾ لَلَبِثَ فِى بَطْنِهِۦٓ إِلَىٰ يَوْمِ يُبْعَثُونَ ﴿١٤٤﴾

"Had he not been of them who glorify Allāh, He would

=

sorry for this life, so he becomes discontented with Allāh's decree in dissolution, going to the hereafter, so one has a bad end and he meets his Lord while he is discontented with Him. It was narrated that the *Shayṭān* is never tougher on a man as in death and he tells his assistants: 'Take this person! if you miss him today you will never catch him again.' We seek refuge in Allāh from his evil, we ask him to bless our death and to have a good end."

[3] Reported by al-Tirmidhī 2516, al-Tirmidhī said it is a good authentic ḥadīth. Also reported by Aḥmad [1:307-308] and al-Bayhaqī in *Shu'ub al-Īmān* and *al-Asma' wa'l-Ṣifāt* p.76. See *al-Durar al-Manthūr* [1:66] and *Tafsīr ibn-Kathīr* [7:91].

have indeed remained inside its belly (of the fish) till the Day of Resurrection."

[*al-Ṣaffāt* 37: 143-144]

Due to the fact that Pharaoh had no righteous deeds, he did not find anything that he could attach to at the time of trial, and so it was said to him,

ءَآلْـَٔنَ وَقَدْ عَصَيْتَ قَبْلُ وَكُنتَ مِنَ ٱلْمُفْسِدِينَ ۝٩١

"Now (you believed) while you refused to believe before and you were one of the evildoers and corrupters."

[*Yūnus* 10: 91]

'Abdul Ṣamad, the ascetic, said on his death bed, "O my Master! For this minute I have kept You [i.e. I preserved Your Mercy so You bestow it upon me at this moment]. Whoever was negligent when in good health will be neglected when sick."

It was narrated that one of the companions saw an old man begging so he said, "This man was negligent regarding Allāh's orders when he was young, therefore Allāh neglected him when he became old."

The cure for this disease is to encourage the self, to tell it that it is simply a fraction of time that will pass and after it will come the complete rest as the Prophet (ﷺ) said, "No anguish will befall your father after this day."[4]

Abū Bakr ibn 'Ayyāsh prayed to Allāh when he was on his death bed and said, "Should I not lay my hope in Him and I have fasted eighty months of Ramaḍān for Him!"

[4] Reported by Ibn-Mājah 1629.

Al-Mu'tamir ibn Sulaymān said, "My father told me, 'O son! Read for me the ḥadīth in which state the concessions of Allāh! So that I meet Allāh while I expect the best from Him."

Therefore a believer should remove fear and steer the camel as a cameleer of the desert said:

Its cameleer gave it glad tidings and said
tomorrow you will see the acacias and the mountains

It was reported that Abū Hurayrah (*raḍiyAllāhu 'anhu*) said, "The Messenger of Allāh (ﷺ) said (that Allāh said), "I am just as My servant thinks I am."[5]

It was also reported that Jābir (*raḍiyAllāhu 'anhu*) said, "I heard the Messenger of Allāh (ﷺ) say three days before his death, "None of you should die except while expecting the best from Allāh."[6]

Al-Fuḍayl ibn 'Iyāḍ said, "Fear is better than hope. However when death befalls, hope becomes better."

I say, that is true because as I have clarified fear is a lash that urges on a lazy person. If a camel is tired then we should use lenience. If one asks what of 'Umar ibn 'Abdul 'Azīz's fear at death, then the answer is, that his fear was a result of his sense of responsibility for his people and the demands of his innate nature over not fulfilling the rights of others. He used to say: "Truly I fear this leadership!" though he used to clinch to the statements of men, therefore, when Ibn 'Abbās told him: "Receive the glad tidings, O Chief of Believers! You were assigned the leadership,

[5] Reported by al-Bukhārī and Muslim.

[6] Reported by Muslim

and you were fair in it and you died as a martyr!" He told him, "O Ibn 'Abbās! Will you testify that before Allāh?"[7]

Section Three: Increase in Anguish

If a sick person increases in anguish, then he should count that as a reward for our righteous predecessors used to like the intensity of the agonies of a sick person because it expiates sins. It was narrated that Ibrāhīm said, "They used to like to be overstrained at death." It was also narrated that 'Umar ibn 'Abdul 'Azīz said, "I would not like that throes of death be eased for me, because they are the last thing that expiates [the sins] of a Muslim."

Section Four: Repentance

A sick person should repent, as long as he is sane, so that he meets Allāh pure from all sins. He should also write his will, put his trust in Allāh, Exalted and Glorified is He, to look after his spouse and children. For He supports and protects the righteous.

[7] Ibn 'Abbās, may Allāh be pleased with them, said this to Amir-ul-Mu'minīn 'Umar ibn ul-Khaṭṭāb when he was stabbed. Aḥmad reported it in his *Musnad* 1:46, and al-Bayhaqī in *Ithbāt 'Athab al-Qabr* through the chain of Dāwūd Ibn Abū Hind from 'Āmir from ibn 'Abbās he said, "I dropped in on 'Umar Ibnul-Khaṭṭāb when he was stabbed. So I said 'Receive the glad tidings, O Amir-ul-Mu'minīn! You converted to Islām when people disbelieved, you fought with the Messenger of Allāh (ﷺ) when others let him down and he (ﷺ) died while he was pleased with you. People did not differ in your *khilāfah* and you died as a martyr." So he said, "Repeat what you have said!" So I repeated it. He said, "By Allāh, the only true God, if I had all what is on earth of gold and silver I would have sacrificed it from the horror of the Day of Judgement."

Section Five: Being Optimistic

If *Shayṭān* bothers a dying person and reminds him of withering away, then he should know that withering happens to the ship after the traveler leaves it. He should also know that the Sharī'ah has stated that a believer is going to live in everlasting delight after death. So whoever possesses true belief should not be sad, because the destination is a good one and whoever does not possess true belief should be sad over not possessing it.

It was reported that Ka'b (*raḍiyAllāhu 'anhu*) narrated from the Prophet (ﷺ) that he said, "The soul of a Muslim is like a bird that hangs on the trees of paradise, until Allāh returns it to the Muslim's body."[8]

The purpose of this chapter is to show that fear of death should be moderate, so that it does not exhaust the body, causing harm, one should fear what is to come after death and work towards it.

[8] Reported by al-Bukhārī in *at-Tarikh al-Kabir* [5:306], al-Ḥumaidī 873, and al-Ṭabarānī in *al-Kabir* [19:64].

CHAPTER TWENTY ONE

Averting Excessive Happiness

WHEN HAPPINESS INTENSIFIES, the blood heats up and hence, it may harm the body, and may lead to the death of he who has excessive happiness if it is not extenuated. If someone sees the way to achieve happiness, he should take the means leading to it. When Yūsuf met his brother, he asked him, "Do you have a father?" and he kept on expressing lenience towards him, in order not surprise him with the good news.

Happiness should be moderate, so that it equals sorrow. If it exceeds the limits, then this is a sign of intense heedlessness. For happiness is unreasonable with a sane person, who is rejoiced by anything that brings joy, but then when he remembers his destiny and the fear of where he will end up, then that joy disappears. If the heedlessness of happiness intensifies it makes a person exultant and reckless. This is why Allāh said,

لَا يُحِبُّ ٱلْفَرِحِينَ

"Surely Allāh does not love the exultant"

This refers to those who exceeded the limits of happiness and became exultant.

The cure for excessive happiness is to think deeply about previous sins and future tribulations.

Al-Ḥasan al-Baṣrī said, "Death has exposed this *dunya* (world). It did not leave any happiness in it for the sane."[1]

[1] *Al-Zuhd* by Aḥmad Ibn-Ḥanbal p.316 through the chain of Ibrāhīm Ibn-'Īsā al-Yashkarī from al-Ḥasan.

CHAPTER TWENTY TWO

Averting Indolence

LOVING LEISURE, PREFERRING idleness and the perceived difficulty of tasks are what lead one to laziness. Bukhārī and Muslim reported from Anas ibn Mālik (*raḍiyAllāhu 'anhu*) that the Prophet (ﷺ) used to frequently say,

« اللهم إنى أعوذ بك من الهم والحزن والعجز والكسل »

"I seek refuge in Allāh from grief and distress, old age and laziness."[1]

Muslim reported in his Ṣaḥīḥ that Abū Hurayrah (*raḍiyAllāhu 'anhu*) narrated that the Prophet (ﷺ) said, "A strong believer is better and more loved by Allāh than a weak believer."[2]

At all times, strive for that which will benefit you, seek the help of Allāh, and do not be helpless. If anything (bad) befalls you, do not say, 'If only I had done such-and-such, then such-and-such

[1] Reported by Bukhārī 8:98, Muslim p.2079, 2080 and 2088 (Abdul-Baqi)

[2] Reported by Muslim, *al-Qadar* 34.

would have happened.' Rather you should say, 'Allāh preordained this, and whatever He wills He does,' for the words 'if only' open the door to Satan.

Ibn Mas'ūd (*raḍiyAllāhu 'anhu*) said, "I detest a man whom I see idle from striving for this world and the hereafter."[3] He also said, "At the end of time there will be people whose best actions will be blaming each other, also known as the lazy ones."

Ibn 'Abbās (*raḍiyAllāhu 'anhu*) said, "Slackening married laziness and they gave birth to poverty."

Mālik ibn Dinār said, "There is no righteous deed except that there is an obstacle that comes before it, if a person endures it patiently he will reach comfort, and if he fears it he will abstain from it."

Sufyān al-Thawrī said, "People left riding fast horses, and we have stayed on indolent camels."

Section One: The Cure for Laziness

The cure for laziness lies in motivating and urging the endeavor by fearing that one may miss the goal, or be blamed, or fall into regret [lest one does not make an effort]. For the regret of a negligent person when he sees the reward of a hard worker is the greatest punishment. Also a person of sound mind should reflect on the negative consequence of indolence, for many a time has leisure lead to regret.

[3] Reported by Abū Nu'aym in *al-Ḥilyah* 1:130, through the chain of Yahya Ibn Wathāb from Ibn Mas'ūd, may Allāh be pleased with him.

Whoever sees that his neighbour has travelled, returning with profits, his regret will be many times greater than the satisfaction of leisure, similarly if one person becomes brilliant in knowledge and another does not due to his laziness. The intended purpose of these examples is to explain that the pain of missing something exceeds the satisfaction of laziness.

Wise people are unanimous that wisdom is not reached by relaxation and idleness. Therefore, whoever knows the fruits of laziness will avoid it, and whoever is aware of the fruits of hard work will endure the hardships of the path. Moreover an intellectual knows that he was not created in vain, rather he, in this world, is like a hired laborer or a merchant.

The span of lifetime in this world, which is practically the life one is given to perform good deeds, and the span of time one is to spend in the grave is like a single moment compared to the eternal dwelling in paradise or in the hellfire.

From amongst the best cures for indolence is reading and reflecting on the biographies of those who strove. Therefore, I wonder at he who would prefer idleness in the sowing season and leaves yielding for the harvesting season.

It was narrated that Farqad said, "You put on the garment of leisure before you started working. Have you not noticed that when a worker starts working he wears his cheapest garment, when he is done, he takes a shower and puts on two clean garments. On the other hand you wore the garment of leisure, before you even started working."[4]

[4] *Ḥilyah al-Awliyā'* 3:47 through the chain of Ibn Shawthab from Farqad al-Subkhī.

CHAPTER TWENTY THREE

Identifying One's Flaws

KNOW THAT THE SELF IS LOVED and the flaws of the beloved might not be apparent to the lover. However, some people are so resolute in their struggle against themselves that they consider their selves as their enemy in opposing it, and so they are able to see its flaws.

Iyās ibn Muʿāwiyah said, "He who does not know his own demerits is a fool!" He was asked, "So what are yours?" He answered, "Excessive talking." However this is very rare, because people usually hide their own flaws, but we do not mean that a person does not know of his flaws, for a person of sound mind recognizes his flaws, I rather mean the concealed flaws. For they are like internal diseases that a doctor does not know of, and so cannot prescribe a medicine for, because they do not have symptoms. Also a person's love for himself prevents him from viewing his hidden flaws as flaws.

A poet said:

The eye that looks with contentment does not see flaws,

But the eye that is full of discontent sees all flaws

It was narrated that a man accompanied another and when he wanted to leave him he said, "Tell me about my flaws." The man answered, "Ask anyone other than me for I have been conceiving you with the eye of contentment."

If someone asks if flaws are concealed and a person does not regard them as flaws, then how can we identify them? The answer is that there are seven methods to overcome this:

The first method: A person should take the wisest, most prudent of all the people he knows as a friend, ask him to tell him about his flaws and inform him that in doing so he does him a favor. Then, when this friend tells him about them he should rejoice in that, and should not show any sadness, so as not to encourage his friend to stop telling him about them. He should inform his friend, "If you hide anything from me I will consider you a cheater."

The second method: He should search for what his neighbours, brothers, the people he deals with, to inform him about him, what they praise him for and dispraise him for.

The third method: He should find what his enemies say about him, for an enemy always tries to find the flaws of his enemy. Taking this point into consideration, a person will be able to benefit from his enemy in a way that he cannot benefit from his friend, and that is because an enemy mentions one's flaws but a friend hides them. Thereafter a person will avoid those flaws.

The fourth method: He should imagine that someone else has his characters, then he should choose what he likes of those characters and leave the objectionable ones.

The fifth method: He should reflect on the consequences and fruits of his different characteristics so that he comes to know the good that results from the good characters, and the bad that results from the objectionable ones. That is due to the fact that honest reflection is both very powerful and insightful.

The sixth method: To measure all his deeds by the Shar'īah, have them reviewed by insightful persons, measure them in the scale of justice, for it can distinguish between what is better and what is worse.

The seventh method: He should read the stories of those who acted upon their knowledge and then measure his actions against their actions, thus he would even regard the effects of a shortcoming as a flaw that he should avoid, let alone the performance of a bad deed.

CHAPTER TWENTY FOUR

Motivating a Low Endeavor

IF THE DEFECTED ENDEAVOR is an established habit of the self, then no cure will have any effect on it. However if it is acquired as a result of accompanying those with low endeavor or because of the predominance of the nature or desires, then its cure is attainable through many ways; some of them include: boycotting the people of low endeavor, disdaining them, accompanying those who have high endeavor. Then reflecting on the consequences, the destiny of those possessing low endeavor , and the destiny of those who are serious and hard working. As 'Abdul Ṣamad said, 'A man who was known for his hard work died while people were still saying to him, 'Die today so that you may live forever', and this statement awakened me.'

Whoever thinks deeply about people of high endeavor will know that they are no different from him, when it comes to what they are created from, them being human beings, however the love of idleness, leisure has aggrieved and chained him. So they have walked away while he stood still, if he had moved the foot of determination, he would have reached what they reached.

A poet said:

> If you like the characteristics of a person,
> then imitate him and you will be what you have liked.
> For there is no barrier before
> generosity and good morals if you come to them.

He who reads the biographies, stories of the righteous predecessors will find that most of the jurisprudents and scholars are from amongst the slaves, the weak, or those with low craftsmanship, but as their endeavors were high they succeeded. If people with low endeavor contemplate the consequences of their low endeavor, they would understand that their idleness is their enemy, however, they have favored low endeavor, hastening relaxation and leisure. Further, their regret for losing virtues, people's disrespect, humiliation is indeed greater than every distress and adversity. In contrast, the people of high endeavor receive comfort through others dignifying them, and the elevation of their status in this world as well as in the hereafter, which removes the bitterness of the hardship endured. It is as though he who endured hardship never relaxed, and he who relaxed never endured hardship.

It was reported that Anas ibn Mālik (*raḍiyAllāhu 'anhu*) narrated from the Prophet (ﷺ), "One of the inhabitants of the hellfire who had the utmost pleasure in this world will be brought forth on the Day of Resurrection and will be dipped into the hellfire. Then he will be asked, 'O son of Adam! have you ever seen anything good?' Have you ever enjoyed any pleasure?' He will say, 'No, by God, O Lord. Then one of the inhabitants of paradise, who had the most miserable life in this world, will be brought forth and will be dipped into paradise. Then he will be asked, 'O

Son of Adam! Have you seen any misery? Have you experienced any adversity? He will say, 'No, by God, O Lord! I have never suffered from any misery and I have never seen any adversity."

The meaning of this ḥadīth is that exhaustion and the bearing of hardship will end, only comfort remain. On the other hand comfort and ease will end, and only remorsefulness remain. For life is just a season [that will end], the loss is blocked, yielding is urgent, and some of this is enough to disturb the sluggard.

CHAPTER TWENTY FIVE

Self Discipline

THE BASIC PRINCIPLE is that mankind's nature, disposition is sound and healthy. Whereas disease and defects are extraneous, every child is born upon the *fitrah* (natural disposition), which is further explicated in knowing that discipline is ineffective except in an intellectual, thus it does not benefit a mule, and a wild animal that is looked after while young, will not leave hunting when it matures. And you know of the famous story, 'who informed you that your father was a wolf?'.

Know that within every human being there exists three capacities: A lingual capacity, a lustful capacity, and an anger capacity. That said, he who Allāh honored by bestowing upon him the love of knowledge should care for perfecting his 'lingual self', by which Allāh favored him over all animals, and with which he shared a common characteristic with angels. He should make this self capacity predominant over the other two capacities. So that it becomes like the rider, his body becomes like the horse, because a rider should be predominant over a horse due to his elevation, so he be able to lead it wherever he likes and he should be able to slaughter it if he so wishes. Likewise the lingual capacity should be predominant over the other two capacities, using and ceasing to use them as it likes and whoever is like that truly deserves to be called a human being.

Plato said: "A true human is he whose 'lingual self' is stronger than the rest of his other types of selves, because if lustfulness is excessive, a person becomes an animal. If a person releases his *Hawā*, lives an unrestrictive life, then he becomes displaced from his centre, hence he will become worse than an animal, because that is actually the nature of animals, but, in his case, he has contradicted his [humanly] nature. And when the anger capacity is excessive, humans' traits become as that of wild and beastly animals. Hence, one should tame his inner self by opposing lustfulness, controlling anger and following the lingual capacity, so as he may become like the angels and avoid worshipping lust and anger."

Section One: How to Discipline Oneself

Know that discipline of the self is achieved through lenience and moving from one state to another. This should not be done violently but rather leniently, and then he should combine both hope and fear. He strengthens this discipline by keeping good company, leaving bad company, studying the Qur'ān, beneficial stories, thinking about paradise, hell and reading the biographies of wise people and ascetics.

Some of the righteous predecessors would desire a sweet treat, and so they would promise themselves to eat it. If they prayed the night prayer they would allow themselves this reward.

Sufyān al-Thawrī used to eat whatever he desired and then when he woke up in the morning he would say: "The black man has fed his child!" Scholars and exegetes have always been and continue to be lenient to the self until they have owned and subjugated it.

A neighbour of Mālik ibn Dinār said, "One night I heard him saying to himself, 'That's how you should be!' The next morning I told him, 'There was no one home with you, so who did you say that to?' He said, 'Myself asked me for some bread, it insisted so I restrained it from eating for three days, then I found a dry piece of bread, when I was about to eat it I said, 'Wait I will get soft bread' so it [his self] said, 'I am contented with this.' So I said, 'That's how you should be!"

Know that if the self knows that you are serious it will also be serious and hardworking, if it knows that you are indolent it will become your master.

A poet said:

> A horse rider knows the characteristics of his horse,
> so he exhausts it repeatedly, by making it sense fear.

From among the practices of discipline of the self is bringing it to account for every statement, for every action, for every negligence and sin. When its discipline is over, it will appreciate the exhaustion it endured.

Thābit al-Banānī said, "I endured the night for twenty years [by praying] and [then] I delighted in the night for twenty years."

Abū Yazīd said, "I kept driving myself to my Lord while it cried, until I drove it while it smiled."

A poet said:

I still laugh and weep every time I look
Until its eye is tainted with my blood

Nevertheless one should not forget the rights of the self, which is giving it its gratifications that do not oppose the object of discipline. For if it is prevented from its aims in general, the heart will become blind, worries will disperse, and the slave will become constrained. And know that the estimation of the self with Allāh, May He be exalted, is greater than the estimation of the acts of worship. This is why He has permitted the breaking of the fast for a traveler; however it is only the people of knowledge who understand this.

CHAPTER TWENTY SIX

Disciplining Children

THE BEST OF DISCIPLINE IS that which is done at a young age. On the other hand, if a boy is left to his own characteristics and matured possessing these characteristics, then changing him would be difficult.

A poet said:

If you straighten the branches they will straighten up,
but wood does not soften if you amend it.
Discipline benefits children gradually,
but it will not benefit those who have aged.

Perseverance in discipline is a significant principle, particularly in regard to children as it benefits them in that good becomes a habit to them.

A poet said:

Do not neglect disciplining a child,
even if he complains of the pain of exhaustion.

Know that a doctor considers the age of the patient, his place, time and then he prescribes the medicine. Likewise discipline should be suited to each child, and the signs of the success or failure of a child can be noticed from a very early age; a clever child is stimulated by learning and the unintelligent is not availed by learning similar to the way a camel tamer does not become intelligent by practicing sport.

A man once told Sufyān al-Thawrī, "We hit our children if they do not pray." Sufyān told him, "You should rather [encourage them and] give them glad tidings."

Zubayd al-Yāfī used to tell the boys, "Whoever prays will have five walnuts."

Ibrāhīm ibn Adham said, "O Son! Seek the knowledge of ḥadīth. I will give you one Dirham for every ḥadīth that you hear." So on account of this he started to seek the knowledge of ḥadīth.

Section One: Taking Care of the Trust

A father should know that his child is a trust placed in his hands, so he should make him avoid bad company from a young age. He should teach him the good, for a child's heart is empty and accepts anything that is given to it. He also should make him love shyness and generosity. He should make him wear white clothes. Thus, if he asks to wear colored clothes then he should tell him that these are the clothes of girls and effeminates. He should tell him the stories of the righteous, make him avoid love poetry, because it is a seed of corruption, he should not prevent him from reading poems about generosity or courageousness, so that he exalts these characteristics and becomes courageous.

If he makes a mistake he should overlook it. His teacher should expose his secrets and mistakes, he should not reprehend him except in private. He should prohibit excessive eating, excessive sleeping, make him accustomed to simple food, minimal sleep for it is healthier. He should be treated with physical exercises such as walking, disciplined by being prohibited from turning his back to people and from sneezing and yawning in their presence. If he chooses to exhibit a bad characteristic, he should be deterred from it excessively before it becomes a habit, and it is fine to discipline him if lenience is of no use. Luqman told his son, "O Son! Disciplining the son acts as a fertiliser for sowing seeds."

If the boy is aggressive, his father should be lenient with him. Ibn 'Abbās said, "The aggressiveness of a boy is an increase in his intelligence."

Section Two: Future of your Child

Wise people used to say, "Your son is like your flower the first seven years, and your servant the second seven years. By the time he reaches fourteen, if you have been good to him then he will be your partner, and if you were bad to him then he will be your enemy." A child should not be beaten or offended after he reaches puberty, because then he will hope to lose his father in order that he may have his own way. Whoever reaches twenty years of age and has not become righteous, then his godliness is remote, however leniency should be practiced with everyone.

CHAPTER TWENTY SEVEN

Disciplining and Handling Wives

IT IS NECESSARY TO STUDY this chapter thoroughly, for the worthiest of acts is that a man marry a virgin, who has not known a man before him.

Wise people have said, "A virgin is for you, and a non-virgin is against you." Further, it is a grave mistake for an aged man to marry a young girl, for she will become like an enemy to him as he will not be able to fulfill her needs and as her needs are not met she will naturally develop an aversion towards the old man. Thus, if a man is tested with such and has married a young woman while he himself is aged then he should treat her aversion with good morals, tolerance and by spending money on her extravagantly.

This has already been explained in detail in my book *'Al-Shayb'* (Grey Hair [Old]). One should also beautify himself for his wife just as he likes that his wife beautify herself for him, he should cover his body so that she does not see from him anything except that which is liked and she should do the same.

Section One: Acts which lead the Wives Astray

A husband should not joke with his wife often, so that she does not belittle him and hence become disobedient. Moreover he should not place all his money in her hands, so that he is not placed under her control as she could take his money and leave him. Allāh, May He be exalted, said,

وَلَا تُؤْتُوا السُّفَهَاءَ أَمْوَالَكُمُ الَّتِي جَعَلَ اللَّهُ لَكُمْ قِيَامًا

> "And give not to the foolish your money which Allāh has made a means of support for you."
>
> [*al-Nisā'* 4: 5]

Rather he should joke with her, while maintaining his prestige and status.

Section Two: How to discipline a Spouse

The best way to discipline a woman is by preventing her from speaking with other women (who are not righteous, who possess evil traits and morals) and from leaving the house (unnecessarily). Further, an elderly woman should be assigned to discipline her, teaching her how to respect her husband, informing her of the rights of a husband, also to dignify in her eyes he who spends moderately, and act as her preserver for the insanity of a youth is dangerous.

Section Three: Marrying concurrent to One's Age

If an aged man marries a woman who is not a young immature girl, nor an old feeble woman, then that would be better for him as she would be less arrogant and more respectful towards him.

Section Four: Needs of a Young Man

A young man demands what he wants, he cannot be enforced to do what he does not like, therefore if he wants to enjoy women then it is a choice he can take i.e. he could buy young slave girls, if he is able to. This is because young (slave) women do not have jealousy or, at least, they do not possess it excessively, because they are owned and because of their owner's ability to replace them and sell them. He, however should assign a keeper to monitor them and also have another keeper to observe the already assigned keeper.

Section Five: Being Content with what one has

If a man is granted a woman who is exactly everything he desired, he should forget what he missed for the sake of what he has, because branches are never mentioned when the origins and roots are preserved, also having an excessive amount of women requires a lot, the least of which is taking care of them.

CHAPTER TWENTY EIGHT

Disciplining and Handling Family and Slaves

KNOW THAT IF YOUR FAMILY notices that you have surpassed them in wealth or social status, they will begrudge you. However, since deserting them is prohibited, one should then deal wisely with them for it is a critical matter i.e. being good and kind to them, without informing them of that which is unknown to them. From the worst mistakes when dealing with family members is to grant some of them and deprive others. Nonetheless, whoever chooses to do so, should strive incredibly hard to conceal this from them so that they do not detest him as a result of that.

As for slaves, in actual fact, they own their masters, because they are the ones who administer their masters' food and beverage, therefore a person should be kind to them so that they do not wind up murdering him [i.e. poisoning his food or drinks]. Bizr Jamhur said, "We are the kings over our people, and our servants are the kings over our souls, and there is no way that we can be fully cautious of our servants, therefore we deal with them wisely and go along with them. A king should keep his prestige with them, while being lenient towards them. However he should be even kinder to them, particularly those who are in charge of his food and drink." Also know that if the slaves are smart, they may hide some secrets from you and so they might cheat you; on the other hand if they are foolish then you will not benefit from them, because they will not understand what you want and so will not be able to fulfill your needs. The correct procedure is to employ the foolish ones inside the house and the smart ones outside the house as this will ensure that all wants and aims are fulfilled safely.

Section One: Being Cautious

It is also a grave mistake to allow a teenage slave boy to enter the house, particularly if he is attractive and there are women in the house, for if they do not fall for him, he might fall for them. Further, it is a risk to leave a pubescent boy among slave girls because the intensity of sexual desire and the ignorance of youth makes one forget the magnitude of the prohibition.

These are fundamental rules that should be remedied with their cures, and should not be left to continue until they bring about worse circumstances.

CHAPTER TWENTY NINE

Consorting with People

SINCE PEOPLE'S NATURES are varied and different, getting along with everyone is difficult. For this reason, the best that a person of sound mind can do about this is to seclude himself and keep himself to himself, for this is indeed generates a great comfort and relief. Nevertheless, if he has to associate with people then he should do so in a kind manner while being lenient towards them, fulfilling their rights, ignoring his own due rights, he should be patient with those who are ignorant, forgive those who are unjust, and give the arrogant the best seat in a gathering. The best means by which he can attain their affection is through forgiveness and bestowals. Besides, by these two, he can enslave those who cannot be led. It was mentioned in a ḥadīth, "Dealing wisely [going along] with people is a charity."

Section one: Associating with Laypeople

If a scholar is tested with associating with laypeople, then he should be very cautious, as lay people's aims and purposes are different to those of a scholar; what makes one of them contented makes the other discontented. And some of them are angered by correctness because they see it as wrong; and, in spite of their ignorance, they do not accept what the scholars say.

Therefore a scholar should distance himself from them as much as he can, because associating with them brings dishonor to him, belittles him in their eyes and so his knowledge becomes disparaged by them. Further, if a sinner sees a scholar laughing or eating, or if he hears that he got married, then he will not have any respect for him [i.e. they may think of him as someone seeks worldly pleasures and not the hereafter]. Therefore one should be very cautious of them, for such people are actually the killers of the Prophets. However, if he has to socialise with them, then he should not say much to them, and he should speak not what they may take advantage of, or of anything that might not be suitable for him to speak about with them. After incorporating all this, assuring safety from them is possible.

CHAPTER THIRTY

Flawlessness of Character

THE SIGNS OF A FLAWLESS PERSON are: being upright and disciplined by the Capacity of Allāh from an early age, a faculty for wise, resolute opinions, decisions, and an expansive mind while still young. Allāh, Exalted is He, said,

وَلَقَدْ ءَاتَيْنَآ إِبْرَٰهِيمَ رُشْدَهُۥ مِن قَبْلُ

> "And indeed We bestowed aforetime on Ibrāhīm, his (portion of) guidance."
>
> [*Anbiyā'* 21: 51]

Ensure he has high endeavo, is of noble character that motivates him to pursue high endeavors, and prevents him from pursuing low ones, therefore when he plays games with children during his childhood, such a person always likes to be the leader of the other children. Thereafter when he grows up, good morals will be his emblem without him even learning them, shyness, and bashfulness will be his garment without it being forced on him. The least of discipline will have an effect on him, just as a grindstone benefits steel but does not benefit iron.

Afterward, when he reaches the age in which he can reason and knows the signs that prove the existence of his Creator, when he comprehends why he was created, reflects on the statements he was addressed with, his final destination, and the point of it all; then he will work hard, knowledge will reveal to him the reality of things and so he will understand that the best of matters is that which brings him closer to his Creator. He will also know that the best of that which brings one closer to the Creator is knowledge and acting upon it, so he will strive to accomplish as much as his body can bear, he will awaken the intention and the endeavor to accomplish the rest.

Though you find some people who confine themselves to certain fields of knowledge, for example one studies only grammar his entire life, another studies only ḥadīth, he on the other hand knows that all types of knowledge are important, therefore, as he knows that life is too short to encompass all knowledge, he learns and takes what he needs from all fields as supplies for his quest, he works in accordance with this knowledge, and so he profiteered from his time fearing that it might pass without him reaching his goal. He therefore does not waste a minute in anything that is not useful, and he even takes advantage of the time he uses to eat and sleep as he knows that the period [he is given] is very short.

As a poet said:

So accomplish your goals quickly,
for your age is nothing but one journey of many.

And race like race horses and be the first,
for they are loaned to you and you shall return them.

Such a person is always striving to fill his time [with beneficial deeds], he subjugates his *Hawā* to reform his matters, he learns only beneficial knowledge because his heart is distracted by correcting his objectives from amusement and his bodily parts are seriously devoted to Allāh and His obedience. One is content with what Allāh has given him and does not beg from people, he abstains from their money to protect his honor, and so he becomes better than them because he is self-sufficient, he removes their corruption with his advice and admonishment.

Thus, when he does deal with them it is with justice and fairness, he will elevate himself over them due to his rank, if they ask for his advice he does his best to advise them, nevertheless, he is diverted from everyone else by his desire to reform himself as he is ready for his transfer [from this world to the hereafter] his only concern is packing his luggage [good deeds], so he guards every second and strengthens himself with plentiful supplies, because he knows that his journey is long. Then one strives to reform knowledge in his life, so that his legacy will remain after his death.

He also abstains from this world and only eats the amount that is necessary to carry him through his day. If he allows himself more than what is necessary from a permissible matter, then his aim is to make his camel strong enough to bear him. He remains in the grace of his Lord until all that made him truly love Him, hence he becomes devoted to Him, and relishes His way so that when he is with people, he is with them in body only, however his heart remains constantly with his Creator.

Such men are Allāh's favorites on His earth, the seekers [of the pleasure of Allāh] breathe their air and the fragrance of their truthfulness is exuded after they are laid in their graves, for there is prestige in their graves that tells the status and rank of each one of them. When their deeds are mentioned, a seeker is strengthened by them on his path of patience. On the Day of Resurrection, the Righteous who fear Allāh are the stars of the sphere while they resemble its sun or its full moon.

May Allāh grant us the ability to imitate them, may He grant us their rank and may He bestow upon us their morals by His vast grace, for He is the All-Hearer, He is close to His slave. May the prayers and peace of Allāh be upon Muḥammad, his family, and his companions.

www.ingramcontent.com/pod-product-compliance
Lightning Source LLC
Chambersburg PA
CBHW051901090426
42811CB00003B/422
9781643544151